more praise for *Idea Stormers*

"As a creative thinking expert, I am very familiar with Bryan Mattimore and his outstanding work in the ideation and innovation consulting field. Bryan is one of the best facilitators and corporate creativity consultants in the world. He is among my heroes who inspire, teach, and guide others in the corporate world on how to create original and implementable ideas that make a difference in our competitive business environment. Mattimore's newest book, *Idea Stormers*, offers a host of creative-thinking tools and techniques. More importantly, it provides an excellent framework for unleashing the creativity of groups, no matter what their role or function is within an organization. Mattimore's behind-the-scenes look at his successes with teams provide you with lessons and techniques to create, inspire, facilitate, and drive creative collaboration to generate the ideas you need to achieve uncommon results. Alone we can do so little; together we can do so much. Mattimore shows us how together we can generate original ideas, make good ideas great, and create game-changing ones."

—Michael Michalko, author, *Thinkertoys, Cracking Creativity, ThinkPak* and *Creative Thinkering*

■ ■ ■

"Question everything! Hands-on and ready-to-go, here are techniques to get you started."

—Seth Godin, author, *Purple Cow*

■ ■ ■

"Bryan Mattimore has helped me create breakthrough new products for Godiva, generate innovative promotions for The Food Network, and most recently, with re-positioning *Good Morning America*. I know firsthand that the ideation techniques and innovation processes in *Idea Stormers* work, and that they can unleash the creative potential of any team. *Idea Stormers* should be required reading for anyone on the front lines of marketing innovation!"

—Adam Rockmore, senior vice president marketing, ABC Daytime and News and SOAPnet

idea stormers

how to lead and inspire creative breakthroughs

bryan w. mattimore

JOSSEY-BASS
A Wiley Imprint
www.josseybass.com

Jacket design by Adrian Morgan

Author photo by Tim Geaney

Cover Illustration © Michele Paccione, iStockphoto (RF)

Published by Jossey-Bass

A Wiley Imprint

One Montgomery Street, Suite 1200, San Francisco, CA 94104-4594—www.josseybass.com

Jossey-Bass books and products are available through most bookstores. To contact Jossey-Bass directly call our Customer Care Department within the U.S. at 800-956-7739, outside the U.S. at 317-572-3986, or fax 317-572-4002.

Wiley publishes in a variety of print and electronic formats and by print-on-demand. Some material included with standard print versions of this book may not be included in e-books or in print-on-demand. If this book refers to media such as a CD or DVD that is not included in the version you purchased, you may download this material at http://booksupport.wiley.com. For more information about Wiley products, visit www.wiley.com.

Library of Congress Cataloging-in-Publication Data

Mattimore, Bryan W.

  Idea stormers : how to lead and inspire creative breakthroughs / Bryan W. Mattimore. — 1st ed.

    p. cm.

  Includes bibliographical references and index.

  ISBN 978-1-118-13427-6 (cloth)

  ISBN 978-1-118-22517-2 (ebk.)

  ISBN 978-1-118-23870-7 (ebk.)

  ISBN 978-1-118-26329-7 (ebk.)

  1. Creative ability in business. 2. leadership. I. Title.

  HD53.M3744 2012

  658.4'092—dc23

                                                                    2012022687

Printed in the United States of America

FIRST EDITION

HB Printing   10 9 8 7 6 5 4 3 2 1

To my wife, Hazel, who is creatively brilliant without even trying.

contents

preface

Some years ago, quite by accident, I happened upon my young daughter, Caroline, standing in front of the mirrored armoire in our dining room. Caroline was dressed in a beautiful princess outfit with a royal crown on her head and a magic wand in her hand.

As I watched her stare at herself in the mirror, I was immediately struck by her intensity. This was not, by any stretch of the imagination, just child's play. This was serious business. I watched and waited, unseen, curious to see what she would do next. And then, to my surprise, even though she was alone, she said something.

"I have a magic wand," she proclaimed to her reflected mirror-self in an utterly determined voice, "and I am not afraid to use it!"

To this day, I still feel blessed to have witnessed such a moment of pure imagination and creative willpower in the life of my child. Over the years, as I've reflected on what my daughter said that day, I've come to see that it has great symbolism for both the work I do and this book.

I'm convinced that the insights, stories, advice, and creativity and innovation processes in this book can become a sort of magic wand for both individuals and leaders of high-performing teams. You have in your hands the work of a dedicated practitioner who, day in and day out, for over thirty years now, has been confronted with the creative (and often daunting) challenge of helping clients generate more and better ideas to solve critical business challenges. So at one level, there is nothing theoretical about the content in this book. These are accounts of what actually happened: stories of the creative mind-sets, processes, and techniques that helped generate breakthrough ideas and solve difficult creative business challenges. Essentially these are stories of what *worked*.

However, telling stories of what worked is not enough. I've also shared the why of my work: specifically, why I believe a particular creative approach, technique, or mind-set was effective for a challenge. My hope is that with these explanations, you will arrive at a broader theoretical understanding of the creative processes themselves, including which creative techniques are most likely to work best for specific kinds of creative challenges. It's the combination of and linkages among theory, technique, practical application, and results that makes this book different from how-to creativity and innovation books on the market, and I hope it is much more useful.

So welcome to the world of creative idea creation, a world in which you may already be well traveled. Even for the seasoned creative traveler, I'm confident you'll discover original, inventive, and practical new creative thinking tools and techniques, which, like my daughter, Caroline, with her magic wand, I fully expect you won't be afraid to use.

idea stormers

introduction: idea engines

The call came from Candelin Wahl, Ben and Jerry's aptly titled "Mother of Invention." Would I be interested in working with Ben and Jerry's new product development team to design and facilitate a brainstorming session to generate new ice cream novelties ideas: popsicles, bonbons—anything but new flavor ideas for pints? The session would be near Ben and Jerry's headquarters at a Vermont inn, and every flavor of Ben and Jerry's ice cream would be served at the afternoon break as creative inspiration. Would I be interested? "When can I come?" was my response before even thinking about negotiating my fee.

There was a catch though: as part of the day-long ice cream novelty session, I'd also have to lead the group in naming a new Ben and Jerry's ice cream flavor: a delicious new combination of fudge and strawberry ice cream. Sure, I could do that. I'd done scores of naming sessions before. *No problem,* I thought.

But in fact, yes, there was a problem. Candelin said we could devote only half an hour to naming the new ice cream—even though the new product development team had already been working on the name for over three months without much success. So could I do it in half an hour? No way. As an experienced naming session facilitator, I knew we'd need more time if we were going to have any chance of success.

Candelin was insistent, though, and I finally relented. Yes, I'd figure out a way for the group to name the new strawberry and fudge concoction in half an hour.

I was aware that I'd have only one shot at it. The creative technique I'd create would have to get everyone in the session thinking very differently, and very quickly. I also knew that the technique should be stimulus rich: triggering people's brains with a variety of thought prompts—either words or pictures—to inspire a new creative connection.

Could I use a random collection of artists' illustrations as inspiration or expressions from a database of popular headlines? How about showing clips of some of the funniest TV commercials of all time as the idea starters? What about using creative greeting cards as stimulus? Award-winning children's books? A dictionary of imaginary places? Or maybe I should try passing out lists of famous quotes? Or *New Yorker* cartoons?

None of them felt right, so I let a few days go by, giving my creative subconscious the space and time it needed to address this design challenge. Time has a way of helping clarify the most important strategic components, or essences, of a creative challenge. You may discover, as I have, that the most important creative contribution of the subconscious may be less about sparking a "eureka moment" solution and more about clarity for thinking about your creative challenge. With this clarity, the creative solution then often follows easily and naturally.

So with time, the essential question I came to ask myself about the Ben and Jerry's naming assignment was, "What did all these random prompts, even the fun ones like the *New Yorker* cartoons, really have to do with ice cream anyway?" Even more to the point, what did they have to do with the antiauthoritarian, challenge-the-status-quo essence of the Ben and Jerry's brand? My answer: Not much. So this led to my next question: "Is there an ideation technique I can create that will focus on and leverage the essence of the Ben and Jerry's brand?" Even more specifically, I asked myself, "Are there antiauthoritarian words I can use as ideation triggers?" Well, yes, there were. Slang was certainly antiauthoritarian. Risky as it might initially seem, I decided to use slang words and expressions to inspire the group.

So I bought, and then cut up, several slang dictionaries. In the Ben & Jerry's session, I gave each team of brainstormers a dozen or more of the cut-out pages from the dictionaries and asked them to use these pages as thought stimulators to generate four to five new names for our new strawberry and fudge ice cream. Slang expressions like *vidiot, flugie, oofus, fake-bake,* and *V-girl* didn't help much, but one slang expression did. S.N.A.F.U., which typically stands for Situation Normal, All F@%&ed Up, was given a new meaning by the group: Strawberries Naturally All Fudged Up. It was a little edgy, a little silly, a little countercultural—and clearly descriptive of the product. In short, it was a perfect Ben & Jerry's flavor name. So in our case, SNAFU was anything but, and it was the name that launched the flavor.

This Ben & Jerry's naming session was only one of the hundreds of often daunting creative challenges I've had to address and ultimately solve for organizations large and small. As an ideation facilitator and innovation consultant over the past two and a half decades, I've helped hundreds of companies create or name a new product, come up with a new ad campaign or promotional idea, generate a new growth strategy, or even invent a new innovation process.

Idea Stormers gives you a behind-the-scenes look at some of the creative challenges and successful processes that I've used to inspire teams to think more innovatively, no matter what their role or function within an organization. Leveraging the learnings from over fifteen hundred ideation and innovation consulting assignments, I have filled this book with a diverse and provocative palette of empirically validated tools, tips, and techniques to help you and your team create original, but also entirely practical and implementable, creative ideas. My hope is that my explanations of the how, what, and why of many of my company's successful idea-generating techniques and innovation processes will give you both a framework and the confidence to know when and how to apply them yourself, and even invent your own.

the facilitating leader

This book is for the facilitating leader: that is, anyone in any organization, ranging from the CEO to an assistant brand manager to a department leader, who's responsible for addressing and solving creative business challenges. You might be facilitating creative groups directly; participating in ideation sessions; managing, training, or hiring facilitators; or promoting the value of ideation within your organization. I'm confident that anyone in any of these roles, whether a novice or seasoned facilitating leader, a beginner or experienced ideator (or somewhere in between), will find valuable tools and inspiration here.

Many excellent books exist for improving personal creativity. This book has another purpose. The point of *Idea Stormers* is to provide a framework and tools for unleashing the creativity of groups. Group ideation processes, when well designed and well facilitated, are capable of generating a host of highly attractive creative options, and occasionally truly breakthrough solutions, to virtually any business challenge. Well-designed innovation processes can make good ideas great and great ideas game changing.

The challenge is to tap into and channel the power of the collective mind. This is the creative task of the facilitating leader, and, speaking from considerable experience, I can say it is an endlessly fascinating, exciting, satisfying task. Being in the room when the magic starts happening—knowing you helped spark it and that it has the potential to add dramatically to the organization's competitiveness, market share, vibrancy, or bottom line—never gets old.

the innovation imperative

Ideation—the term for the collection of group creativity techniques formerly known as brainstorming—is fun but can be hard work. Innovation—getting an idea or product to market successfully—is much harder work still. Both, but especially innovation, which is complex and with high stakes, can be fraught with highly political, occasionally gut-wrenching, even career-threatening challenges.

New ideas by definition challenge the status quo and bring with them risk and unsettling uncertainty. They can even be seen as highly threatening, especially by those who have a vested interest in the current structures and processes. Enlightened managers who are committed to the future success of their organization often find themselves balancing the company's stated need for new business-building innovations with the organization's natural, and often well-intentioned, proclivity for rejecting the new and mitigating risk.

The manager's apparent dilemma of having to either create the new or defend the successful status quo can be difficult. The reality, of course, is that this either-or mentality of choosing between successfully managing the status quo and innovating the new is not particularly useful. Today's manager must be able to do both. And indeed, successfully managing the status quo in today's intensely competitive, rapidly changing world most likely involves generating new ideas just to keep up. So whether you consider yourself an innovative, trail-blazing pioneer or someone who's tending to previously settled territory, the ability to creatively solve problems and generate creative new ideas, and inspire others on your team to do the same, will be an essential skill set of every successful manager in the future, not just marketing or advertising managers or R&D directors.

Creating the new is not only about creating revolutionary marketing campaigns or breakthrough new product ideas. New ideas are needed to address every imaginable kind of organizational challenge and at all levels in every department, including human resources, manufacturing, sales, customer service, strategic planning, logistics, trade relations, accounting, and legal. I know this to be true because our clients have asked us over the years to address creative problem-solving challenges in every one of these functions. Whether you need to create a better sales forecasting system in the automotive industry, or find a way to decrease disability claims in a luxury goods company; whether you have to reduce the turnover of department store beauty advisers of a cosmetics company, or reduce automobile congestion in the City of New York, creative problem solving is the same for seemingly noncreative organizational challenges as it is for generating a $100 million new product idea or an award-winning ad campaign. It's all about making new connections between related, or even (previously) unrelated, elements to create new ideas and options.

leveraging organizational creativity

Potentially the most valuable, but arguably the least leveraged, asset of any business is the creativity of its employees—all of them. This truth came home to me quite forcefully in early 2002 when I was preparing to lead a creativity and innovation workshop for managers at Consolidated Edison, New York City's electric power company. To help me design the workshop, I asked that I be allowed to visit several power substations, as well as ride the trucks on repair calls. On the morning of my day-long field trip, I put on my Con Ed hard hat and climbed in the truck with Mo, a twenty-year veteran of the company. Mo drove us to our first repair call in midtown Manhattan, where I soon found myself wending my way through the catacomb-like, subterranean passageways at Rockefeller Center looking for leaks in hundred-year-old steam heating pipes. It was a lot of fun, though I had two serious questions I asked every employee I spent time with that day, starting with Mo:

- "What's the one thing you would do to improve the work you do?"
- "In all of your years working at Con Ed [several of the workers I interviewed had more than thirty years with the company], what are you most proud of?"

Of the more than a dozen Con Ed employees I interviewed that day, every one of them, including the thirty-year veterans, said that they were most proud of the creative contribution that they had made to the company. Their creative contribution could have been a simple idea to save the company money, a suggestion to make service calls more efficient, or even a novel approach for designing a large power grid. Mo's simple idea to improve communication with customers, while also helping Con Ed repairmen be more efficient and therefore productive, was to equip each of them with a Con Ed cell phone. Small idea or big idea: it didn't matter. It was the creation of a new idea, any new idea, that gave them the most satisfaction.

It became clear to me that day, riding the Con Ed trucks, that everyone, and I mean everyone, has the potential and, if encouraged, the desire to contribute new ideas to help their company. Successful managers of the future must recognize this. Learning and using the simple creativity techniques and innovation processes in this book will dramatically add to any manager's ability to inspire the creative potential in themselves and their coworkers. In the process, not only will they help themselves and their company grow and become more profitable, but they will also make their organization a much more dynamic, interesting, and, dare I say, fun place to work. Just ask Mo.

about idea stormers

Ideation is a creative enterprise, and like any other art, it has tools and traditions—and openings for something new to burst through. This book contains tips, tools, stories, principles, best practices, hypothetical situations, and thought experiments—a dozen different angles on the central question: How can you channel the creative thinking of a group to yield the best solutions to business challenges?

The chapters of this book move broadly from theoretical to practical, though practice and theory are intertwined in every chapter. In Chapter One, I explain certain creative mind-sets that can help you realize more of your inherent creativity and creative potential. I move on in Chapter Two to a simple and useful categorization of the most effective techniques and then in Chapter Three to a description of what I consider to be the seven best ideation techniques of all time that can help you and your team ideate that next breakthrough idea.

In the middle three chapters, I show different aspects of creating, managing, and thinking about a successful innovation process. Innovation—making an idea operational—is where the rubber of the good idea meets the road of real-world circumstances. Chapter Four gives an overview of the successful innovation processes that my company has pioneered on behalf of our clients in over two hundred innovation consulting assignments. In Chapter Five, you'll find specific process recommendations for generating and innovating ideas for classic creative business challenges such as inventing and naming new products or services, developing unique and ownable brand positionings, and creating more effective promotion, advertising, and trade marketing ideas. This chapter also includes discussions of strategies and techniques my clients and I have used to address such traditionally noncreative business activities as developing competitive business strategies, forecasting sales, and transforming a culture to make it more innovative. Chapter Six covers some of the common challenges that even great ideas meet when you begin moving them toward implementation and how to creatively navigate these complications without losing focus on your ultimate goal.

The last three chapters are about facilitating others on your team to be more creative in group ideation sessions. Here I provide strategies and recommendations for combining the tools, techniques, insights, perspectives, mind-sets, and approaches in this book with the actual work of facilitating. Think of these chapters as counsel and guidance on how you can become a true facilitating leader within your own organization. Chapter Seven is intended to guide your thinking in the who, where, and how of an ideation session. Chapter Eight describes, step by step, a new product ideation session that extends over a day and a half. And my goal in Chapter Nine is to empower you with five strategies to help you invent new ideation techniques and innovation processes to solve unique, or even seemingly intractable, creative challenges.

With commitment to innovation and ideation, your organization can become an engine of creativity and growth. After reading *Idea Stormers*, I believe you will be fully prepared, both psychologically and practically, to use it to start leading yourself, your team, and your organization to unparalleled levels of growth and success. Let's begin!

1

a map of the creative mind
embracing seven creative thinking mind-sets

A re there certain mind-sets that help both individuals and teams to create more and better breakthrough ideas? And do some creative mind-sets work better than others for solving different kinds of creative challenges?

Yes.

This chapter identifies these creative mind-sets and explores how you can apply them to inspire your own creativity as well as the creativity of those with whom you work.

the seven creative mind-sets

I've identified seven creative mind-sets, although unlike the typical list of things, they do not fall easily into neat and discrete categories. Indeed most of these mind-sets are anything but discrete. The inherent messiness of the creative process means that at any time, they can, do, and probably should overlap. Such is the modus operandus of the creative mind: discrete categories often give way to creative continuums.

Curiosity

Curiosity is creative mind-set number one. It tops the list because without curiosity, the creative process never has the raw material it needs. Think of a young child who persistently, and even obnoxiously, asks, "Why?" Or consider the story of Thomas Edison visiting Louis Pasteur at his home. Pasteur had a sign-in guest book that included not only space for the guest's name, but his or her area of interest as well. After signing his name, Edison wrote for his area of interest, "Everything."

So if we can bring the young child and Thomas Edison together, we'll be continually asking "why" about everything. Of course, this is not a creative mind-set that most adults can or want to keep going for any length of time. The adult mind quickly tires of asking, "Why?" either because it feels it already knows the answer or because it seems immature and a waste of time to question everything. However, a judicious use of our childlike curiosity can pay enormous dividends, as we will see throughout this book with some of the creative techniques that embody and leverage the curiosity mind-set.

Openness

Creative mind-set number two is an active and creative openness to others and their ideas. Thinking this way can be viewed as quieting the opinions of the judgmental mind long enough to allow the creative mind the time and space it needs to generate interesting insights, associations, or connections. If curiosity is about continually wanting to learn new things, an active and creative openness is the willingness, indeed the desire, to process these new learnings in ways that open up creative possibilities as opposed to superficially categorizing them into self-limiting dead-ends. To give a broad example, labeling the guy you don't agree with a jerk may make you feel better, even superior, but it doesn't do anything to inspire your own creative process. Keeping your mind open to that guy and his ideas—even if he and they are irritating you—may not be easy or comfortable, but it can lead to inspiration and insight.

Embracing Ambiguity

Embracing ambiguity is the third creative mind-set. Related to, but different from, maintaining an active and creative openness, it is the capacity to entertain contradictory, ambiguous, or incomplete information. It was the brilliant (and self-contradictory) writer F. Scott Fitzgerald who said that "the test of a first rate intelligence is the ability to function while simultaneously entertaining two contradictory ideas." This is not easy to do, but it's critical to success in the creative process. To the controlling mind-set, contradictions are a source of discomfort, even anxiety. To the creative mind-set, contradictions are an invitation to more focused creative thought. More than a few of my marketing colleagues, especially when they're behind the glass viewing focus groups, want to jump quickly to an answer, because they cannot deal with the discomfort caused by the psychological messiness of ambiguity. Ironically, it's often by working the ambiguity, that is, delving deeper into the apparent contradictions and ultimately resolving the paradox inherent in seemingly contradictory ideas, that a new, unambiguous, integrated, and occasionally brilliant idea may emerge.

Finding and Transferring Principles

The fourth creative mind-set is principle finding/principle transfer. As its name implies, this creative mind-set has two parts. The first part is the mental habit or discipline of continually identifying the creative principles inherent in an idea, especially (but in no way limited to) the new ideas in your field. Inventors look to understand what makes a breakthrough invention revolutionary, screenwriters the elements that make an award-winning script so compelling, chefs what makes a new combination of foods so delicious. You get the idea. But the most creative people also look to other fields for inspiration. In fact, if you look at the history of the creation of paradigm-shifting, breakthrough ideas, they tend to come from either the young or people who were trained in a different field. Philo Farnsworth was thirteen years old when he conceived of the basic operating principles of electronic television, and he transmitted the first television image when he was twenty.

And Alexander Graham Bell, after inventing the telephone, went on to cofound the National Geographic Society.

The second part of the principle finding/principle transfer mind-set is adapting the identified principle or idea to another context to create a new idea. It's the ability to work from the bottom up, moving from the specific to the general—a facility for abstracting principles or ideas from something specific, and then applying it in a different or more general way to something else. Psychologists and scientists call this mind-set *inductive thinking.* Call it *adapting, transferring,* or even *stealing* from one arena to create something new in a different arena. Henry Ford got the idea for mass-producing his cars from a visit to a slaughterhouse. (Think assembly versus disassembly.) Samuel Colt came to the idea for his six-shooter revolver by noticing the clutching mechanism of a turning ship's wheel. And Eli Whitney, in conceiving the cotton gin, made the connection between a cat reaching through a fence trying to grab a chicken and "claws" spreading out cotton so that a "fence" could more easily knock off or separate the seeds from cotton.

Searching for Integrity

Creative mind-set number five is the search for integrity. It's the desire to discover, and the belief that there exists, an insight or connection that will unite the seemingly disparate elements you're juggling in your creative mind into a single integrated, conceptual whole. When it happens, it's exciting and magical, and it feels absolutely, positively, and completely right. Everything just fits. Einstein would call it "beautiful." Enough said. Integrity doesn't need to explain itself.

Knowingness

Knowingness is creative mind-set number six. This is not the knowingness that accompanies the moment of connection in mind-set number five, the search for integrity. This is the knowingness that you bring with you from the beginning of the creative challenge through the difficult, even seemingly impossible challenges and inevitable creative deadends you encounter along the way until you make the creative breakthrough. My business partner, Gary Fraser, and I call it "knowing that there's a there there." It explains in part creative persistence. It's the confidence to know that with enough creative attention, focus, and effort, sooner or later you'll solve your creative challenge.

Knowingness is such an important creative mind-set because like success, creativity is a self-fulfilling prophecy. To see this connection, substitute the word *creative* for *successful* in Henry Ford's famous quote, "Whether you think you'll be successful or not . . . either way you'll be right." In my world, we know we'll get new ideas if we put enough attention and focus on the creative challenge, even if it's for such seemingly mundane, and therefore often very difficult, new product development assignments as inventing new envelope ideas; creating a new ratchet, wrench, or socket set; or developing a new line of laundry detergents.

World Creating

Finally, creative mind-set number seven is creator of worlds, and it is the most purely imaginative of the seven. It's the province of novelists, game designers, screenwriters, fashion designers, all children, and delusional mental patients. Think of the created worlds of *Star Wars,* Ralph Lauren's Polo, the video game World of Warcraft, Dr. Seuss, Harry Potter, all sports, Hunger Games, cloud shapes, *Lord of the Rings,* Salvador Dalí, Candy Land, *The Matrix,* and dreams. It's the ability to imagine entirely new worlds and everything in them, including the rules that govern those worlds. It's imagining original places, people, and things with unique designs, time frames, personalities, emotions, "feels," and mind-sets. It even involves role-playing roles that you yourself may write.

training your creative mind

There are of course other creative mind-sets. These just happen to be my personal magnificent seven. One I didn't mention, for instance, is "think the opposite." The preferred creative mind-set of bankers, lawyers, anarchists, and teenagers, this mind-set is pretty much self-explanatory. I say "white"; you say "black." I say "yin"; you say "yang."

Now consider this: even an in-depth understanding of each of the now eight mind-sets I've discussed above won't help you or your team much when it comes time to actually create a breakthrough idea. The reason is that being creative isn't about understanding the creative states of mind that facilitate creativity. It's about being creative. And that act of creation occurs most often, and most successfully, when the mind goes beyond its left-brain, analytical, self-conscious mental constructs to achieve a kind of transcendental moment where unexpected, even magical creative connections occur. In sports, it's called "being in the zone." And when you're in the zone—let's say you're a tennis player—you're not debating with yourself whether you're holding the racket with the right grip, wondering if your shoulder is facing in the right direction, or thinking that your feet might be too far apart as you are about to make a winning backhand volley. You're too busy doing, with very little conscious thinking about what you're doing.

Think of descriptions of creative mind-sets, creativity-spurring techniques and tips, and even stories about the creative process (all of which you will find in this book) as part of a kind of creative-thinking training program. You can consciously learn about them, train yourself in their application, and even use them to become conscious of the processes that you do naturally or unconsciously. Then, with repeated contact and attention to them, you will begin to internalize them. But even if you never fully internalize them and have to always self-consciously apply them, it doesn't matter. At the end of the day, you will still have the benefit of generating new, occasionally breakthrough ideas from their application.

In training psychology, a shift from this self-conscious, overly mental, and enforced reasoned thinking to a much less self-conscious, more natural, often effortless, in-the-moment doing, is called moving from conscious competence to unconscious competence. For most people, with enough exposure, training, and practice, different creative mind-sets, like a well-practiced backhand volley, will become automatic.

They become so much a part of your everyday thinking style it'll be easy to believe you always thought that way. And you'll be right. As kids, we were all creative geniuses. We just may have forgotten how truly creative and original we were so naturally and so unconsciously.

If you're skeptical of your former creative greatness, take a moment and review each of the creative mind-sets above with the innocence of the five-year-old child who used to be you. With a little retro-creative imagination, I believe you'll discover that in some way, you exhibited each of these eight creative mind-sets. For instance, if I revisit my five-year-old self, I can see me riding a sawhorse in the neighbors' back yard chasing bad guys in the Old West. That sawhorse was as real to me as any actual horse I'd ever seen on TV. A "sawhorse" into "real horse"? Yes, because I knew there was a pony in there somewhere. It's a good example of the creative mind-set of principle transfer. Or is it the creator of worlds mind-set? Could it be both? And if it's both, shouldn't we also include the embracing ambiguity mind-set?

I believe you'll see that these creative mind-sets are in there. They always have been and are available to all of us. With a little reeducation and retraining, you can rediscover these creative mind-sets and then eventually, and somewhat ironically, unconsciously practice them, just as you did as a child.

So how do you get started, consciously training yourself and those you might be leading creatively in these mind-sets? If you go back to mind-set number one, curiosity, you'll have your answer: it's by asking more and different kinds of questions:

- In the case of the curiosity mind-set, for instance, all you have to do is keep asking, "Why?" or maybe, "How does that work?"
- For the openness mind-set, you might ask, "What's the learning here?"
- For the embracing ambiguity mind-set, you could ask, "What can resolve this apparent contradiction?" or maybe, "If both of these contradictions are correct, what ideas might they imply?"

- For the finding and transferring principles mind-set, you can ask, "What's *the* principle in this thing that I can apply to *that* thing."
- For the searching for integrity mind-set, your question might be, "What would make this a simple or beautiful solution?"
- For the knowingness mind-set, you might ask, "What's my intuition telling me?" or possibly, "If I already knew the answer to this creative challenge, what would the solution look and feel like?"
- In the creator of worlds mind-set, you could ask, "If I were to enter an entirely new world, what would I imagine that world would look, feel, smell, and sound like? And what might the rules be that govern this new world?"

a meta-creative mind-set

As you practice the seven (actually now eight) creative mind-sets by asking yourself and your team more and better creative questions, consider one last mind-set. This one is embodied in all of the previous ones, so you might think of it as a kind of meta–creative mind-set.

What helped me realize the enormous creative potential of this meta mind-set was an e-mail with the subject line, "Contact from Colombia." I'm still surprised that I even opened this e-mail, but when I did, I discovered an interesting proposition. It was from Hans-Peter Knudsen, the president of Colombia's oldest and most prestigious university, University of Rosario, located in Bogotá and founded by Spanish missionaries in 1653. Before becoming the university's president, Knudsen had been a business professor who had used my first book, *99% Inspiration*, to help educate his classes about business creativity and innovation more than twelve years before.[1] Because innovation had become such a hot business topic in Colombia, he was proposing that he represent me and my company to Colombian businesses, associations, and government institutions. In due course, I agreed to a series of meetings, speeches, and innovation workshops for the presidents of some of Colombia's most important businesses and government institutions. One such speech was for the

Colombian Association of Flower Growers and Exporters, known as Asocolflores.

I flew into Bogotá on a Wednesday night, and Peter gave me a detailed briefing over dinner on the business challenges facing Colombia's flower growers. I learned that two out of every three flowers bought in the United States is grown in Colombia, but that because of the devaluation of the Colombian peso, the Colombian flower growers were suffering. Other flower-exporting South American and Central American countries with better exchange rates with the United States were making it very difficult for the Colombian flower growers to compete.

That night at the hotel, I realized that the innovation speech I was planning to give the next morning might fall on deaf ears. Not that my innovation process suggestions wouldn't be of value for inspiring longer-term innovation successes. They certainly would. But these growers might not have the luxury of planning for the longer term. They were in a battle at the moment for their very survival, with tens of thousands of employees' jobs on the line. They needed to quickly generate short-term solutions to address their exchange rate challenge.

As I thought about the flower growers' problem, I realized that one way to address their pricing dilemma was to somehow add value to their flowers to justify a higher cost. It was a classic case of decommoditizing a product, that is, one being bought and thought about only in terms of price.

So the creative challenge, as I defined it, was, "What could be added to the flowers to increase their perceived value to American consumers?" It was this simple question that led me to generate the twenty creative growth strategies that I would recommend in my speech the next morning. The question would also help me ultimately recognize both the existence and the creative potential of a profoundly simple meta–creative thinking mind-set.

In a word, you could call this creative thinking mind-set "AND." You simply add an "AND" to whatever you need a new idea for. Said another way, you ask yourself what you could combine with the creative challenge you're working on to bring it, and your thinking, to a new place. So for the flower growers, the question was, "Flowers AND ____ would make flowers more valuable?"

Often when I have a creative challenge, I commit to generating as many as twenty ideas. Having an idea quota ensures that you will not stop creating when you get what you think is your first good idea. I've also discovered that the first good idea is rarely the best one. Usually the first five ideas, in a twenty-idea quota, may be okay or even quite good. But they also tend to be the obvious ones. Ideas six through fifteen are often a little further out. Several of these may even be great ideas. But ideas sixteen through twenty really push your thinking to explore nonobvious, sometimes counterintuitive, even absurd or crazy ideas. It's the freedom that craziness provides that can lead you to create the best ideas of all.

So that night before I finally fell asleep at 3:00 A.M., I forced myself to generate twenty creative, idea-generating strategies for the flower growers, all based on the AND mind-set. Here are the AND creative strategies, as well as several of the concrete ideas that they suggest for adding value for the Colombian flowers:

1. Sports	11. Contracts
2. Fundraisers	12. Historic events
3. Food	13. Promotions
4. Trends	14. Luxury goods
5. Personal identity	15. Celebrities
6. Education	16. Celebratory tool/milestones
7. Sales/selling tool	17. New distribution channels
8. Hobbies	18. Emotions
9. Travel	19. Greeting cards
10. Institutions/companies	20. Religion

For instance, the "flowers AND sports" strategy might lead to the idea of marketing boutonnieres in the colors of a winning sports team: black and orange flowers for the San Francisco Giants, blue and white flowers for the Dallas Mavericks, and so on, sold in these teams' home cities. The "flowers AND food" strategy might suggest linking specific colors and kinds of flowers to specific dishes at fine restaurants to bring an added aesthetic to the dining experience. The "flowers AND contracts" strategy might suggest championing a discounted, frequent-purchase yearly contract with heavy flower-buying individuals and companies. "Flowers AND historic events" might inspire the idea of creating a special 9/11 flower that could be used as a fundraiser for victims' families. The "flowers AND religion" strategy could lead one to think of offering a new series of birthday bouquets for, say, Catholics that included a biography of a Catholic saint born on that same day. And so on. It's not hard when you move from a creative mind-set of thinking about either-or to one committed to "AND." It's also a lot of fun.

This "AND" creative mind-set helped me create one of the most effective speeches I have ever given. It was clear from the Colombian flower growers' reactions and their in-depth conversations with me after the speech that they liked my suggestions. They also greatly appreciated my having taken the time to customize my more general innovation process suggestions to address their specific and immediate business challenge.

So that's it on the creative mind-sets. Again, think of them as a kind of backdrop or foundation for all the stories, techniques, and creative principles you'll encounter in the rest of the book. You won't find them explicitly tied to particular challenges or techniques, but they are always in play whenever creative business challenges are addressed. Knowing them—having names for them and choosing when and how to exercise them by asking the questions associated with them—will inform and inspire your and your team's creative process and results.

In the next two chapters, we look at group ideation techniques: in Chapter Two, a framework for conceptualizing the most effective techniques, and in Chapter Three, a discussion of the techniques themselves.

2

beyond brainstorming
understanding individual and group ideation techniques

Here's a joke from a cynical client:

> *Question:* What's the difference between a brainstorming session and an ideation session?
> *Answer:* An extra two thousand dollars a day for the facilitator.

There's some truth in what the client says, but it's also true that there is a big difference between brainstorming and ideation. *Brainstorming*, still generally used as a catch-all term to describe group idea generation, is, strictly speaking, only one of several hundred specific idea-generating techniques. The term *ideation* took its place in the business lexicon because a categorical term was needed to describe all the new group and personal idea-creation techniques that have been developed since the invention of brainstorming in the late 1930s.

The technique of brainstorming was invented by Alex Osborne, the "O" in the advertising agency BBDO. Since advertising in the late 1930s was (and still is) a business of ideas, Osborne was continually trying to invent new ways to inspire his staff to generate more and better ideas on behalf of their clients. In countless idea-generating sessions, he began to notice two important psychological group dynamics.

First, he realized that teams often wanted to quit creating too early. Creative teams were typically looking for the "one right answer" or "that one big idea." And once they got what they thought was that big idea, they'd stop. Mission accomplished. Osborne had the idea to keep his creative teams going: rather than settle for the first or even second "great idea," they would shoot for a half-dozen, or even a dozen or more, "great ideas." So one of the fundamental principles of his newly invented group brainstorming technique became this: quantity of ideas leads to quality of ideas. The second, and in some sense more important, psychological factor that Osborne noticed is that session participants' criticism of an idea tended to discourage—and in some cases completely shut down—further creative idea building. Why did this happen? It was because people took the criticism of their own ideas personally.

The best brainstorming sessions are those where participants feel comfortable and safe psychologically, verbalizing what I'll call "idea intuitions." An idea intuition may be a vague feeling, an idea fragment, or even a more fully fleshed-out idea that could sound crazy or even stupid. It's easy to recognize these idea intuitions because session participants invariably will preface them with an excuse like, "This may sound crazy but . . . ," or, "This is probably a really stupid idea but . . . ," or even, "I'm not quite sure what I'm even saying here but . . . " As a facilitator, when I start hearing idea intuitions, I know that the session is coming together. It means that the participants have moved beyond having to justify either themselves or their ideas to the others in the group. They are trusting one another enough not to have to verbalize fully fleshed-out or even "logical" ideas.

Conversely, when a participant starts to feel defensive in a brainstorming session—because someone might have criticized one of her "crazy" ideas—it starts to shut down the session. Trust begins to dissolve, and with a loss of trust, the idea building that is so critical to the success of a session—that is, the reason that the participants have been brought together as a group—also starts to disappear. This was the psychological insight that Osborne had back in the late 1930s and why the second fundamental tenet of brainstorming is to withhold judgment during the creative phase of the brainstorming session or, to put it another way, separate the idea-generation stage from the idea-selection stage.

In its day, the technique of brainstorming was an important advancement in the process of group idea generation. Even today, the principles of withholding judgment and quantity equaling quantity are important and valid. Newer ideation techniques build on those principles but also include even more powerful creative practices.

brainwalking: in search of better brainstorms

In the past twenty-five years, I have facilitated over a thousand ideation sessions. The techniques I use in any one session vary widely depending on the creative task. The design of a strategic visioning session, for example, will be very different from that for a new product ideation session, and a creative cost-cutting session design is not even remotely similar to a positioning ideation session. You might be surprised to learn, then, that I believe that 80 to 90 percent of the time, there is a single best technique to use to begin an ideation session, regardless of the creative task or desired outcome. This technique is similar to and has many of the pluses of Osborne's brainstorming technique, but it also has some critically important differences and advantages. The technique is called *brainwalking*, and I invented it, out of necessity, when doing work on a large chewing gum project several years ago.

Brainwalking has a close cousin, *brainwriting*, which helped lead me to the creation of brainwalking, a kind of written idea exercise that is simple to learn and facilitate. Brainwriting begins with presenting the creative challenge and giving a piece of paper to each participant in the session. Each person writes down an idea for meeting the challenge on a blank sheet of paper and passes his or her paper to the next person, who then builds on that idea or uses it as a stimulus to trigger a new idea. Papers are usually passed four to five rounds. So if there are twelve participants in a session and five rounds of passes, you end up with sixty ideas. After the final round, each sheet is returned to its original owner, who then circles one or two favorite ideas to discuss and build on with the group as a whole. That's it. Don't let the simplicity of the technique fool you. It's a profound and powerful technique with important psychological and group dynamic ramifications. Most obvious, the group using this technique generates a great number of ideas very quickly. Contrast brainwriting with a typical brainstorming session, in which one person throws out an idea, another builds on it, and yet another person builds on that build. One person talks, and everyone else listens. It's not a particularly efficient or effective way to get a lot of ideas out quickly.

Brainwriting also allows people to share from the start any ideas that they may have thought of before coming into the session. It's important to get those ideas out early because someone may well have a great idea, and you certainly don't want to either overlook the idea or not have the opportunity for the group to develop the idea further. Sharing these ideas is also important because you want everyone open to the process of creating new ideas with the others in the room. If they're preoccupied with one of their own ideas and waiting for the "the perfect time" to present it, they're not fully engaged in the process of creating new ideas.

Another shortcoming of Osborne's brainstorming is that as a group goes down certain avenues or streams of thought, it becomes increasingly difficult for them to get back to the new, and potentially naive, points of view that people may have had coming into the meeting. The group and its participants quickly begin to know too much. One of the wonderful advantages of brainwriting is that there are as many idea starting points as there are people in the session, which is great because you don't know which starting point might lead to a breakthrough idea.

Brainwriting also gets around what I call the introvert/extrovert problem in brainstorming. How many times have you been in a meeting where you wish the extrovert loudmouth who is saying inane things would shut up so that the brilliant introvert in the corner who hasn't said anything yet would get a chance to speak? In brainwriting, everyone gets equal time to "speak" in a nonthreatening way: with their pen. It's a pure and fairly concise form of creative democracy.

From the standpoint of group dynamics, brainwriting is also modeling the behavior that is so critical to the success in the rest of the ideation: idea building and piggybacking. Each time the paper moves to the next person, people build on other participants' ideas and in this way fulfill the true intent of the meeting: generating better ideas through mutually stimulated creativity. Otherwise everyone could simply e-mail their idea, and no one would have to bother to get together as a group. Clearly brainwriting is a powerful way to start an ideation session.

Brainwalking is even better.

Brainwalking evolved out of an ideation sessions I did for Trident and Dentyne gums, both owned at the time by Warner-Lambert. The assignment in the first ideation session was to generate innovative positioning and marketing ideas for Trident. I used the brainwriting technique to start the meeting, and it worked well, even better than I had expected.

A week later, I was slated to facilitate the second ideation session, this time for Dentyne. My problem was that several of the people who were attending the Dentyne session had also been in the Trident session, and I didn't want to start the session with the same exercise. I had to change the act so that session participants would continue to feel excited about and engaged in the process because we were doing something entirely new.

My dilemma was that I wanted a technique other than brainwriting to start the meeting, and yet as a technique, it was tough to beat. After much creative struggling, I had an idea that now seems both simple and obvious: move the people instead of the papers.

I began the Dentyne ideation session by taping large sheets of flip chart paper on the walls around the room, which I called "ideation stations." I gave everyone a marker; then each person went to an ideation station and wrote an idea at the top of the paper. Next, I had them rotate to their neighbor's paper and add an idea, just as they might in brainwriting. After five rotations, I had them return to their original sheet and circle one or two of their favorite ideas.

It's pretty straightforward and didn't seem much different from brainwriting. But somewhat to my surprise, I found that brainwalking had several important and powerful advantages over brainwriting.

For one, the sheer act of getting people up and moving increased the energy in the room significantly. Some people think better on their feet. (Hemingway certainly thought he did. He used to write standing up, with his typewriter on top of his bureau.) In any case, it's an energizing and fun way to start the day.

Also, the ideas in brainwalking, unlike those in brainwriting, are public, and public is a benefit in an ideation session. It's reinforcing for the participants to see dozens of ideas on the walls after only a few minutes of work. I'll never forget what one client said to me, only half-joking, shortly after a brainwalk: "Hey, it's Miller time! Look at all the ideas we've created in just the first twenty minutes of our session. We can quit now!"

Seeing all the ideas on the wall also creates a sense of shared purpose and group identity, which can make facilitating the rest of the session easier. People are curious about what others wrote. Interestingly, participants often "walk the walls" during the day, and it's not uncommon for entirely new ideas to be triggered by this wall walking.

Another, and absolutely critical, advantage of brainwalking is that it is easy to form mini-teams (usually two people) to brainwalk together. By doubling up people, you get half the number of ideas, but what you might lack in quantity more than makes up for in quality, fun, and energy. Partners can discuss and build on their ideas between themselves at their ideation stations before they write them down, and they invariably create better ideas by working together than they would have on their own.

By using markers and flip chart paper in the brainwalk, participants find themselves literally writing the ideas bigger than they ever could with just a pencil and paper at their tables. And after all, coming up with bigger ideas is what an ideation session is all about.

random versus focused: two main categories of ideation techniques

In the many years since the invention of brainstorming, literally hundreds of new ideation techniques have been invented. If you also consider that ideation techniques are often customized with task or category-relevant stimuli, you could make the case that in actual practice, there is an infinite number of ideation techniques or exercises.

So how should one think of these different ideation techniques? Is there a framework or way of categorizing them that might shed light on the theory and practice of why, when, and how to use them? Well, yes, and the rest of this chapter lays out a useful framework.

One primary distinction that we make in our ideation and innovation consulting work is between what might be called random ideation techniques and focused ideation techniques.

Random techniques are just that: random. Are you trying to invent a patentable new product idea? Why not use lyrics from a Beatles song as inspiration? Looking for creative ways to save money in your manufacturing process? Take a trip to a modern art museum. Random ideation techniques intentionally use completely unrelated stimuli as a way to get everyone in the group thinking differently. For instance, the dictionary, or random word, technique begins by opening a dictionary randomly to any page and using the first word that you see as a thought starter for creating a new idea. I have used this technique when I've been desperate for new product or service names, and occasionally it works.

The challenge with random techniques like mindlessly picking a word from the dictionary is that they are at once inefficient and generally ineffective. Occasional breakthroughs notwithstanding, they can waste a great deal of time and generate frustratingly off-target or non-strategic ideas. In contrast, focused ideation techniques enable the facilitating leader to inspire breakthrough creative ideas for specific creative challenges, often within very tight constraints or realities. With such techniques, today's facilitating leaders are equipped to resolve the essential paradox of applied creativity: generating new ideas that are focused and aligned with strategic objectives yet are also creative and nonobvious and that meet true customer needs. Simply put, focused ideation techniques can produce effective, occasionally great creative ideas quickly and efficiently.

four ways to classify focused ideation techniques

Beyond distinguishing between random and focused ideation techniques, there are other ways to think about or classify techniques that might be useful for today's facilitating leader. Several years after I published my first book on applied creativity, *99% Inspiration*, it became clear to me that indeed there are, and defining these classifications has since proven extremely helpful in my innovation consulting work, not only for knowing when and how to apply a specific technique but also for knowing how to customize, adapt, or reinvent a technique to address a creative challenge.

In addition to basic brainstorming (and its close cousins brainwriting and brainwalking), I have identified four classes of focused and customizable ideation techniques for generating ideas for a wide variety of creative challenges:

- *Questioning:* questioning assumptions, problem redefinition, twenty questions
- *Metaphorical and linguistic:* category analogues and idea hooks, headliner, company takeover, semantic intuition
- *Visual:* picture prompts, magazine rip and rap, collaging, positioning continuums
- *Wishing, role play, and fantasy:* wishing, day-in-the-life, worst idea

I discuss most of these techniques in greater detail throughout this book, including how they have been used to help generate ideas in creative business challenges. However, a deeper understanding of the classifications themselves will help facilitating leaders judge how and when to use a particular kind of technique. For the rest of this chapter, we'll take a closer look at each of the four classes of techniques.

Questioning Techniques

Consider these two quotations:

"The scientific mind does not so much provide the right answers as ask the right questions."—Anthropologist Claude Lévi-Strauss

"My mother made me a scientist without ever intending to. Every other Jewish mother in Brooklyn would ask her child after school: So? Did you learn anything today? But not my mother. 'Izzy,' she would say, 'did you ask a good question today?' That difference— asking good questions—made me become a scientist."—Physicist Isidor Isaac Rabi

In the work of the creative businessperson, not unlike the scientist, success often comes down to a question of questions. Succeeding at business innovation requires creative persistence, and the essence of that persistence is often the ability to continually ask new, useful, and creative questions of yourself and your teammates. Questions can keep you and your team going when you feel like giving up. They can keep you open to new possibilities when you're faced with seemingly impossible dead-ends and keep the experiment and the experimenter in you alive.

On the negative side, questions can also be used to intimidate, deenergize, or debilitate or initiate a process of laying blame, evading responsibility, or finding fault. This means we must be careful with the questions we ask. I prefer to look at the positive side of questions and their extraordinary potential for releasing tremendous creativity.

A great question can carry with itself so many things. Certainly a great question can imply an answer, but it can also provide space for your coworkers to create an answer for themselves and in the process discover their own unique thinking styles and creative gifts. A great question can help you sell an idea, set agendas, and lead effectively. Ultimately great questions can inspire you and your team to achieve results you had only dreamed of because they require an openness to new ideas and improvements throughout the concept development process.

As an innovation consultant, my work is at least as much about asking good questions as it is coming up with creative solutions, and maybe more so. In the world of innovation consulting and creative problem solving, I've come to think of questions in two basic ways:

- Questions that help generate new ideas
- Questions that help frame how to think about a creative challenge as a prelude to generating new, strategically on-target ideas

The first class of questions is about creating as many questions as you can as a way to generate as many possible creative ideas as you can, potentially in a wide variety of opportunity areas. The creative technique of twenty questions does just that. It sets a goal of generating twenty questions before trying to find any answers.

The second kind of questions—which we might call framing questions—is more strategic. The search for these questions will help you discover and ultimately better frame the business challenge you want to solve. Put another way, finding a strategic framing question may be more about trying to create the single best question before you start generating ideas. The rationale for identifying a single strategic framing question is that it can focus your creative thinking in a strategically efficient and productive way.

The challenge is that in the real world, you may have no idea what the right strategic framing question is or even how to get there. Often it's only by jumping head-first into a new assignment, asking as many questions as you can, learning as much as you can, and generating as many questions as you can that you might discover the all-important strategic framing question. In this way, the two kinds of questions can be complementary.

A story I recently heard at a new product development conference is a case in point. The tale was told by John Scully, retired Apple and Pepsi CEO, who gave a keynote speech on some of the key innovation lessons he had learned while he was at Apple and Pepsi.[1] Perhaps surprisingly, it wasn't his experience at Apple but rather at Pepsi that provided this example of the importance of finding a strategic framing question (my language, not his).

Scully started at Pepsi in its research department after having worked for the research firm A.C. Nielsen. At the time, Pepsi was a distant number two to Coke. To help Pepsi meet its innovation and growth goals, marketing and research decided to do a large, ongoing, in-home study with 550 consumers to learn more about what beverages they were consuming and how often, as well as which concepts for new carbonated beverages that Pepsi had in development might have the greatest consumer appeal.

Each week they sent a wide variety of new carbonated beverages to each home. At the end of each week, they picked up the empties to determine which new products had the greatest appeal. More empties for one flavor of soda than another meant greater consumer appeal. Interestingly, in the first week, they discovered that almost without exception, all the flavors, no matter what they sent, had been drunk. So naturally they didn't think these results were particularly helpful because they didn't help the researchers

determine which flavors of carbonated beverages consumers preferred. To get a better read on preferences, they did what any other
smart researcher would do: they repeated the experiment, only this
time sending more product. They got the same result. Each week,
they kept sending more and more product, and to their complete
surprise, they continued to discover that all the varieties of the carbonated beverages were still being consumed.

Eventually the research team realized that they had been asking the
wrong question. The important question wasn't, "Which new flavor of
carbonated beverage do consumers like best?" but rather, as they put it,
"How do we get more fluid ounces of soda in the home?" Consumers, it
turned out, had an appetite for drinking a great deal more soda than
they were apparently accustomed to buying. This simple insight led
Pepsi to create the first-ever sixty-four-ounce, family-sized bottled soft
drink, which ultimately helped Pepsi successfully compete with Coke.

The critical point here is that the number and kind of questions
you ask of yourself and your team is itself a creative exercise. In the
process, you may discover, as Scully and his team did, the actual key
strategic question to ask.

Of course, there may not be just one key strategic question. There
may be many. And in the ideation process, these many strategic questions, or if you like, creative questions, may help you generate many,
many ideas. Following are examples of how each of these kinds of questions can look and build on one another when used on a real-world
creative business challenge.

Not Enough Elevators: Using Lots of Questions to Generate New Ideas
This example was inspired by an actual challenge that shows how important asking a large number of questions can be to the creative process.

A developer builds an office building in New York City. As the
building starts leasing up, he discovers, to his horror, that he hasn't
built enough elevators. He has only four elevators when he really needs
six to handle the expected loads for this building.

In pondering questions he might ask to help him generate ideas to solve his problem, two (neither of them particularly creative) immediately come to mind:

1. Where can we get the extra money we need to put in the fifth and sixth elevators?
2. How can we make the elevators we do have work much more efficiently so we don't have to put in extra elevators?

These two questions would have you believe that the solution rests on either money or efficiency. Right? Not at all. Like the workshop participants challenged to move beyond these first-to-mind questions, it's not that hard to generate less obvious but potentially more creative questions. Here are just five:

1. How can we encourage less use of the elevators, especially at peak times?
2. How can we get people to want to take the stairs?
3. How can we get people up and down the building in other ways?
4. How can we decrease the number of people needing to take the elevators?
5. How can we increase the capacity of the elevators we already have?

And there can be many more.

As you read these questions, it may have occurred to you that an interesting question often implies an interesting answer—for instance:

Question #1: How can we encourage less use of the elevators, especially at peak times? An idea encouraging staggered work hours might quickly come to mind.

Question #2: How can we get people to want to take the stairs? This might lead to the idea of a heart-healthy building, possibly with water stations (or other incentives) at each floor in the stairwells.

Question #3: How can we get people up and down the building in other ways? With a little childlike imagination, you might think of floating people up on balloons to get them to higher floors. Or how about letting people rappel down the sides of the building? Or, for a more practical idea, maybe you could build a bridge from the higher floors of our building to a building next door and use your neighbor's elevators.

Question #4: How can we decrease the number of people needing to take the elevators? Maybe this makes you think of a new leasing strategy. Perhaps the landlord could lease space on the lower floors to the "high-percentage-of-employees-per-square-foot" companies, say, a telemarketing firm, and keep executive, large office, lower-percentage-of-employees-per-square-foot firms on the higher floors.

Question #5: How can we increase the capacity of the elevators we already have? This question might get you thinking about an idea that the nation's leading elevator firm actually implemented. In a creativity training workshop I once facilitated for employees of United Technologies, I had several divisional executives from Otis Elevator in the room. They told me that they had built elevators with more than one story as a way to increase elevator capacity. Elevator cabs were stacked on one another, connected by a stairway, and depending on whether you were getting off at an odd or even floor, you might walk up to the "second floor" of the elevator to get off.

These questions and possible answers make me realize again that none of us, myself included, spends enough time asking enough good questions. We need to be as creative about the questions we ask as we are about the solutions and other ideas we generate in response. If you want more and better answers to your creative challenges, start by asking more and better questions.

The question the actual developer asked that helped him get his answer was, "How can we make the wait for the elevators seem shorter?" Great question! (Might this be our all-important strategic-framing question?) A host of possible answers immediately comes to mind when such an interesting and creative question has been asked. Could he put TVs in the hallways? Event boards? Other forms of entertainment? Ultimately this developer's low-cost solution was to put up mirrors in the hallways. Tenants spent their time primping and preening in front of the mirrors instead of impatiently waiting for the elevator. They even began asking who had speeded up the elevators.

A Better Iron: Finding the Right Strategic Framing Question

A strategic framing question is one that helps you determine how to think about a creative challenge, and it can be critical to the success of new product development ideation. Here's an example of the importance of identifying a creative strategic question, drawn from my own work in new product ideation.

Some years ago I got a call from executives at the ironing division of a well-known appliance company. The assignment, as it was originally framed for me, was pretty straightforward: "Help us invent a better iron." Although it made absolute business sense to frame the business objective this way, I knew that from a group ideation perspective, "inventing a better iron" would be too limiting, so I asked if we could instead frame the session more broadly: "How about if we think about inventing new antiwrinkle devices?" or, better yet, "How about if we invent new garment care devices?"

It was important to expand the frame for inventing. Defining the task as "inventing a better iron" contains a number of assumptions that are built into the problem definition and challenge and thereby make it extremely difficult, if not impossible, to invent a truly new or breakthrough product. This is especially true for engineers who spend most of their time thinking about and designing irons. The word *iron* encompasses too many mental givens.

Contrast this with the problem challenge and definition we ultimately used: "Inventing new garment care devices." It instantaneously liberates the engineers to come up with very different ideas. A traveling suit bag with an inexpensive, lightweight built-in electric humidifier to steam away wrinkles while hanging in the hotel closet probably isn't an idea that would immediately come to mind if you were "inventing a new iron," even though it provides essentially the same benefit to the consumer. The great "iron-y" of working with this much broader garment care frame was that in addition to generating a host of very creative new garment care devices, we were able to create several dozen exciting new iron concepts. And these were concepts that if we had framed the original creative challenge as "inventing a new iron," I'm convinced we would never have gotten to.

There are two lessons from this story. One is that it's a good creative rule of thumb that if you're having trouble inventing something truly original within a category, start by framing your creative challenge with a question that redefines the category itself. In inventing a breakthrough new product within a category, it often helps to begin by ideating outside that category. The broader point is that finding the right framing question can make all the difference to the success of an ideation process. In this case, I was able to spot the flaws in the original framing question based on my experience. All that's required, though, is a commitment to finding the right question. Practicing the creative mind-sets laid out in Chapter One can help you find it, whether by asking a lot of questions and seeing what shakes out (curiosity and openness), challenging yourself or your team to think critically about your assumptions (finding and transferring principles), or simply persisting in the knowledge that the right question is out there (knowingness).

There are three surefire ways to know that you and your teammates have found the right question. First, there will be an energy release and excitement that the initial question won't inspire. Second, entirely new, potentially game-changing ideas and solutions will follow easily and naturally from the right question. And finally, odd as it may sound, no one will care anymore about finding the right question. The knowingness that the right question has been found will mean that not only will your coworkers shout out answers, but they'll also start proposing ways to implement their ideas without any prompting from the facilitating leader.

Metaphorical Techniques

Question: How are these terms connected: *metaphor, association, simile, same as, like, analogy, comparison, similar to,* and *equals*?

Answer: They're all about connections.

Whether you call this way of thinking metaphorical, analogical, or associative, being able to make connections between seemingly unconnected things is one of the hallmarks of creative minds. Aristotle went even further and said that the ability to create analogies is the key to genius. In my work of helping companies create breakthrough new ideas, analogies play a critical role in helping inspire these creative connections.

Thomas Kuhn, author of *The Structure of Scientific Revolutions* (and source of the popular business term *paradigm shift*), said, "You don't see something until you have the right metaphor to perceive it."[2] Here's an example of what, for me and a group of executives, became the right metaphor, at least when it came to perceiving something new. Oddly enough, the creative challenge itself was seemingly anything but creative: "How to create a more efficient work environment."

I was in Memphis, Tennessee. Following a night of ribs and Elvis music and the occasional sound of a train whistle in the distance, I was in the second day of a two-day creativity training session with research and development employees from Schering-Plough. We had just come back from a break after generating new ideas to promote an anti–head lice product. (I had no idea head lice was such a big problem—or such a large market—but I digress.)

The next segment of the creativity training was on how to use metaphors to generate new business ideas. And so, as always, I asked the participants for an actual problem against which I could apply the metaphorical technique. Maybe the group was still thinking about head lice, but for the longest time, no one said anything. Finally a research scientist spoke up: "I've got this problem with my lab. There's no more room in it, and yet I still need to get some more testing equipment in there. Got any ideas?"

Honestly, this is the kind of creative challenge I dread. It feels very close-ended to me. It's more about problem solving than *creative* problem solving. There tend to be only a few answers, most of which can be arrived at by thinking of a list of logical alternatives. It's certainly not like inventing a new product or creating a new promotional or ad campaign, where there are literally infinite creative possibilities.

But what choice did I have? No one else had given me an open-ended creative challenge or opportunity to work on, so I had to keep going. After some suitable disclaimers about how not all techniques work on every creative task, I decided to look for analogies in the world of nature, often a good place to look, especially when you're stuck.

So I framed the question this way: "How does nature deal with not enough room?" or, put another way, "How does nature deal with overcrowding?"

"Famine?" suggested one research scientist. "When herds get too big, food becomes scarce, and members of the herd die. It's kind of self-regulating."

"Okay," I said. "What can we metaphorically make die in his office?"

Blank stares.

"Let's try another metaphor. How else does nature deal with overcrowding?" I asked again.

"Well, I guess fire is one way, right?" said another scientist. "Sometimes areas get so overgrown with brush and fallen trees that it takes a forest fire to clear out the underbrush and make it vital again."

I got one of those wonderful intuitive flashes that there might be something here. "So how could we metaphorically create a forest fire in the office, and if we did, how could this help us?"

After some back and forth, we had our eureka moment. If we metaphorically burned everything in the researcher's lab, what would happen? Everything would disappear, right? So let's pretend we actually did that. If we "burned everything"—in this case, moved everything in his lab out to the hall and decreed that he could bring something into his office only when he needed it—what would happen? For one, he'd have a very much less crowded work environment. But he'd discover what was essential to have in his lab on a daily basis and, even more important, what wasn't. After some good-natured ribbing, the researcher did indeed agree that he probably needed only 50 to 60 percent of what he thought he needed to have in the lab on a daily basis.

This was a very simple idea, and in retrospect, it seems obvious. But that's the way it is with all good creative ideas: they are simple and obvious once you discover them. Could he have arrived at this idea logically? Maybe. Maybe not. Was it more fun using the metaphorical excursion than a logical thought process to get us there? Definitely!

Implicit in this example is a simple four-step process for using metaphorical and analogical thinking successfully:

1. Define the problem and its essence.
2. Generate lists of examples from other worlds that embody this essence.
3. Ask how your defined problem could be solved using the principles inherent in these other-world essences.
4. Generate creative options inspired by these principles.

Here's an example of a human resource director demonstrating this process:

1. There's a communication/morale problem in the company.
2. Identify other worlds or ways of communicating: sign language, smoke signals, telepathy, semaphores, or jungle drums, for example.
3. Ask, "What are the principles inherent in [say] jungle drums, that could help solve the communication/morale problem?" Some of the jungle drum principles of communication are that they are

inexpensive, have a rhythm all their own, have coded messages between sender and receiver, and go everywhere at once, allowing the entire tribe to hear the same message at the same time.

4. Transfer one or more of these principles to generate a creative solution. So an idea that would allow "the entire tribe to hear the same message at the same time" (and, the hope is, improve company communication and morale) would be: "Broadcast over the company's public address system or intranet a celebratory song as a way of announcing good news for the company."

It's a simple process, but be aware that to get the most out of this technique, you will most likely have to try it several (if not many) times before you get an idea you're excited about.

If this metaphorical transfer process is starting to sound a lot like the principle-finding and principle transfer mind-set in Chapter One, you're absolutely correct. However, using metaphors is not the only way to do principle finding and principle transfer. Visuals work, too.

Visuals

You might think of visual techniques as the principle-finding and principle-transfer mind-set on steroids. That's because the part of the brain that thinks in pictures often doesn't need a step-by-step process to make analogical connections between visual representations and a seemingly unrelated creative challenge. There is a part of the brain that can sense and make creative connections almost instantaneously—certainly way before the conscious, analytical, or verbal mind can even put into words the solution that the intuitive mind is feeling.

In my company's creative consulting work, we have found that visually oriented techniques have a unique capacity for quickly bringing to the surface intuitionally inspired insights, strategies, opportunity areas, and even new product ideas. Visual techniques can be particularly useful in the early stages of research and new product development. Among the techniques we use most often in our work are those we call picture prompts: YouTube video triggers, customized movie clips, magazine rip and rap, and collaging.

Of these techniques, collaging is probably the best known. For instance, one of our clients, Procter and Gamble, often uses consumer collaging to help its marketing teams identify key consumer insights that would be difficult to discover with more linear or rational approaches. A good example of a project we worked on with P&G where consumer collaging was used was a new product assignment for P&G's Clairol's Nice 'n Easy Gray coverage line of hair colors.

Soon after Procter and Gamble bought Clairol, it became clear to P&G's management there was an opportunity to expand the Nice 'n Easy franchise to target women who had gray-resistant hair. Ultimately the insights derived from consumer collages helped the new product development team create Nice 'n Easy's Gray Solution for "long-lasting coverage for resistant grays."

The women we recruited for one-on-one in-depth interviews were asked to prepare before-and-after collages—first how they felt before they colored their hair (when they were really overdue for a coloring) and then how they felt after they colored their hair. This simple exercise turned out to be very powerful. As a male, I was astounded at how startling the contrasts were in their collages. Before hair coloring (and I'm only partially exaggerating here), it looked like the apocalypse; after hair coloring, we had somehow attained nirvana. I'm not sure the men on our team could have ever understood, without seeing these collages, how emotional it is for a woman to get her hair right. One woman crystallized the whole exercise for me when she said, "If my hair doesn't look good, I don't want to see people or even go out. Coloring my hair allows me to feel good about myself, so then I can go out and give back to the world." Hair coloring is a necessary component of giving back to the world? Wow! And here I thought hair color was just chemicals in a bottle, not a genie.

We have also used film or video clips (what we call YouTube video triggers or customized movie clips) to inspire product positioning, promotion, and new product ideas. For example, I used the famous ten-minute San Francisco car chase scene from the movie *Bullitt* to help marketers from Quaker State position their new motor oil. In a new product ideation session for Jan Sport backpack, I used luggage scenes from *National Lampoon's Vacation* to inspire easier-to-carry ideas for backpacks. And for American Express, to generate ideas to promote credit card use at fast-food restaurants, I used humorous You-Tube videos of people trying to order food, not necessarily successfully, at drive-throughs. Typically when I am using visuals, I use these techniques at low-energy points on a day (after lunch or midafternoon). Invariably they have a way of energizing the group in a fun and creative way, seemingly just when they need it the most.

I developed what we call the magazine rip-and-rap technique because we were finding that in an actual ideation session, collaging takes too much time. With the magazine rip-and-rap exercise, we have participants rip out images, words, and phrases from a wide variety of magazines we've placed on their team tables that could inspire a new idea. Then we have pairs of participants post their "rips" around an ideation station in a brainwalk exercise or on a large open wall if the teams are larger. Depending on the creative challenge, we also occasionally have everyone in the room (or possibly two teams with a large number of session participants) group their "rip and raps" so that they either reflect a variety of themes or tell a story. For a company (or division or department) trying to identify its unique positioning, or vision for itself in the world, the magazine rip-and-rap exercise will likely be the most important creative technique of the day. It's always made intuitive sense to me that a company's vision should be inspired by a collection of visuals.

Of course, it's also not always the case that the magazine rip-and-rap exercise will be a primarily visual technique, since we encourage session participants to "rip and rap" words and phrases as well. Indeed, my business partner, Gary Fraser, and I were quite surprised once when he did this technique with a medium-sized public relations firm, especially since we had recently facilitated a similar vision and positioning workshop for a medium-sized design firm, where 80 to 90 percent of the rips were visual. It was the exact reverse with the PR firm: 80 to 90 percent of the rips were words or phrases. It wasn't until after the session that we realized why we had such dramatically different results: the designers were visual people and the PR executives were word people.

The fact that some people are more visual than others means that some visual techniques will be highly successful with some people and not nearly as successful with others. That's okay. If you as the facilitating leader know this, you can plan accordingly and include a mix of techniques that appeals to different thinking styles at different times during the day.

Wishing, Fantasy, and Day-in-the-Life

Of the four classes of creative techniques, wishing, fantasy, and day-in-the-life is the most purely imaginative (think of the creator of worlds mind-set in Chapter One). The ability to wish for the impossible, as a young child might, or fantasize about incredible futures, or imagine a role and then play it out, is what this class of creative techniques is all about. (In Chapter Three, I provide an in-depth discussion of the wishing technique.)

I had been asked to design and facilitate a day-long workshop on group ideation techniques for the marketing department of a large detergent company. I was looking forward to the day because unlike our ideation and innovation consulting work, there wasn't any pressure to deliver a breakthrough new product idea or marketing strategy. We'd be focused on exclusively learning about creativity, ideation, and innovation processes and having fun.

As the marketers filed in for the workshop, it was not hard to see that something was very wrong. I was happy, smiling, and excited, and they looked depressed, unmotivated, and even angry. I took one of the senior executives aside and asked what was going on. I learned from her that the day before, the company had announced a large reorganization. Some people might be reassigned, and others might lose their job. This was not an easy way to start a day of innovative thinking predicated on creative openness and trust.

My planned ice-breaker, while relevant to their world, was not particularly inspiring: "Tell me a laundry memory you have, good or bad." I sensed that talking about a laundry memory wasn't going to do it that day. It had the advantage of setting the stage nicely by being both personal and related to their daily jobs, but it now seemed too tame. I needed something that would creatively shake things up to help move the participants beyond their preoccupation with their own management shake-up. I needed something surprising, crazy, even weird, to open them up to at least the possibility of learning something new and valuable from the day I had planned. I went for weird.

I took a deep breath and began: "To kick off the day, I would like each of you to imagine a day in the life of a sock. To make this work, it's important for you to pretend that you are actually the sock and tell us what you are hearing, seeing, touching, feeling, and smelling. Also, please make sure that your life as a sock includes a trip to the washing machine and dryer. Carol, let's start with you."

I won't kid you. There were some blank stares. And I imagined some inner groans and rolling of eyes (possibly even my own). This exercise was very close to being over-the-top stupid, but as absurd as it seemed, it worked. It was so ridiculous that people starting having fun with it. They talked about the awful smell of one owner's feet ("Doesn't this guy ever bathe?" they asked) and how they felt like itching all the time because this other guy who was wearing them had athlete's foot. They also said they (as socks) liked the "free-for-all" and the sense of "community" they felt "being naked" while "bathing" in the washing machine with other clothes.

In retrospect, I think what made this technique work was that it forced the participants to get outside themselves. By role-playing a sock, they were able to forget their own concerns, at least for the day, and focus on something that ultimately freed them to think very differently about new products they could invent for the laundry.

Role playing is also a simple but powerful way to identify with a target market consumer, or even gain insights into the shortcomings of products, like a sock or a laundry detergent. It can also be a way to reinvent training, as I learned from a project I did with a large disability insurer.

In addition to the new product and service ideation sessions I did for this insurance company, I was asked to design and facilitate a creative session to help their employees who handled disability claims do an even better job of empathizing with the claimants. It seemed only natural to me to design the day with a series of role-play exercises enabling employees to act as if they had many of the disabilities that their clients had experienced: loss of the use of their hands, arms, or legs; chronic back pain; and so on. It was an extraordinary day, and I know that many of the employees who experienced these role plays were changed forever. Indeed, the experience was such a powerful one for so many people that the company ultimately created a special training program with the role-play technique as the keystone of the training for disability-claimant and customer service employees.

Both wishing and role playing have the unique capacity to help session participants arrive at unique, often surprising, and occasionally breakthrough creative ideas. By replacing traditional problem solving and idea generation with the (imagined) creative approaches of others (role playing) or their own, naturally creative inner child (wishing), session participants will discover they can create entire new worlds of opportunities.

■ ■ ■

So these are the four classes of ideation techniques: questions; visuals; metaphors; and wishing, fantasy, and role-playing techniques. Brainwalking, you could say, is a fifth class of technique, since it truly is in a class all by itself.

It can get very interesting when techniques from different classes of techniques are combined to inspire entirely new techniques and approaches. For example, if you're trying to invent a healthy new snack food, you might combine the magazine rip-and-rap exercise with role playing and wishing by having your team members pretend they are a specific target market consumer and rip out all the things (say, from a health food magazine) they might wish for in a better-for-you snack.

For now, though, let's build up your basic ideation technique tool kit by learning how and when to use what I consider to be the seven greatest ideation techniques of all time.

3

your ideation tool kit
the seven all-time greatest
ideation techniques

O f the scores of ideation techniques we use in our innovation consulting, there are seven that we use more often than any others.
Indeed, these "super seven" typically make up as much as 60 percent or
more of our session plan designs. So by learning these seven techniques,
the facilitating leader can relatively quickly attain a high level of skill
and expertise in both ideation session design and facilitation.

The seven techniques are questioning assumptions, opportunity redefinition, wishing, triggered brainwalking, semantic intuition, picture
prompts, and worst idea. All seven also have the advantage of being:

- Easy to learn and facilitate
- Easily customized to address different kinds of creative challenges
- Diverse enough to leverage different thinking styles and modalities,
  which often produce different kinds of ideas

Let's find out more about each one and how to apply them to
address specific, real-world creative challenges.

questioning assumptions

Imagine that you have just been promoted to category director for all oral care products at Unilever. You have three toothpaste brands in your portfolio: Aim, Pepsodent, and Close-Up. Together they have a thirteen-point share of the billion-dollar toothpaste category, where each point equals approximately $10 million in sales. You're in one of the most competitive categories there is, with two of the toughest competitors on the planet in Procter & Gamble and Colgate. Together the Colgate and Crest brands control over 65 percent of the category and are spending tens of millions of dollars a year in advertising and promotion. What do you do to compete?

When my business partner, Gary Fraser, took over the oral care business at Unilever, he quickly realized that he could not compete with Colgate and Crest in a traditional way. As he put it so well, "They owned the game: the players, the field, the refs, everything. And I certainly couldn't outspend them, so I knew the only way I could compete was to somehow change the game."

How do you change the game? It took seven years of hard work for Gary and his team to create a new product that eventually gained a 15 percent share of the toothpaste category, representing over $150 million in annual sales. They did it by questioning the assumptions in every facet of the business. They questioned assumptions about toothpaste packaging, the price consumers were willing to pay per ounce, how toothpaste was displayed, and how it was advertised.

The product Gary and his team launched nationally in 1993 was the first baking soda and peroxide toothpaste, called Mentadent. For the innovation and his innovative leadership, Gary was named Marketer of the Year by Brandweek. And as Gary readily acknowledges, these extraordinary successes happened because he and his team were willing, indeed encouraged themselves, to question their assumptions at every stage of the new product development process.

Mentadent took advantage of what we would today call a kitchen remedy, a kind of poor man's toothpaste. Since the late 1800s, dentists had recommended that their patients mix baking soda and peroxide, inexpensive and widely available ingredients, to clean their teeth and protect their gums. Mixing these creates a chemical reaction that releases oxygen, which has a healthy effect on the gums. Although the benefits of mixing baking soda and peroxide were well known, no one had been able to figure how to create a stable mixture that could be marketed in a toothpaste tube. And so Gary and his team questioned the assumption that toothpaste had to be marketed in a tube. They created a unique dual dispenser that kept the baking soda and peroxide separate until the two streams were squirted out of the dispenser and combined on the bristles of the toothbrush.

The second assumption they questioned was that consumers were not willing to pay a premium for a healthier toothpaste. To compete in the highly competitive toothpaste category, they would need to be extremely competitive on price, at or below that price of Colgate and Crest. But to justify the added expense of the packaging and the lower dollar return per square foot of retail space (since the Mentadent dispenser was much larger than a toothpaste tube), the cost per ounce of toothpaste in the Mentadent product would need to be marketed at literally twice the cost per ounce of toothpaste of Crest or Colgate. Getting the pricing-to-value equation right is certainly one of the key challenges of successful new product creation, and from all appearances, Mentadent had gotten the pricing very wrong. The Mentadent team's exhaustive consumer research had revealed, however, that there was a highly motivated segment of consumers, "orally concerned adults" they called them, who understood the importance of gum health, went to the dentist regularly, and, most important, were willing to pay a significant premium for the healthy gum benefits that Mentadent offered.

Another set of assumptions that the team questioned had to do with the idea that Crest "owned the dentist" in advertising. For many years, Crest had leveraged its endorsement from the American Dental Association (ADA) to great effect, and as a result, it had become the number one brand in the toothpaste category. Mentadent had no such endorsement. But the Mentadent team questioned the assumptions that they needed the ADA's endorsement and, more important, couldn't in some way leverage the positive therapeutic aura of a dentist in their advertising by coming up with a creative idea. The solution: they secured endorsements not from dentists but the wives of dentists who were using the product based on their husband's recommendation. The award-winning commercial included the line, "My husband's a dentist, and he would never recommend a toothpaste for me that wasn't good for my teeth and gums!"

The Mentadent team went on to question many other product and category assumptions. One, for instance, was that consumers don't like or don't want to buy refills. By writing very clear and easy-to-understand refill instructions, the team created what became the most successful refill in the history of the health and beauty care aisle.

So how might you use the questioning assumptions technique with your team? It's a simple three-step process:

1. Decide how you want to frame your creative challenge. See Chapter Two for thoughts on how to approach this.
2. Generate twenty to thirty assumptions you might be making, true or false, about that creative challenge.
3. Pick several of those assumptions, and use them as thought starters and creative triggers to create new ideas.

Let's say the creative challenge is to generate new ideas to increase the sales of women's electric razor sales by 30 percent (an assignment we worked on a number of years ago). These are some of the assumptions one could make about selling women's razors:

- Mostly women buy women's electric razors.
- A razor is bought primarily for what it does.
- To make money in this category, the electric razor needs to retail for at least $29.95, and preferably $35.95 or more.
- Our target market is women ages twenty-five to forty-nine.
- Women buy razors primarily for shaving their legs and underarms.
- Electric razors should be designed to last for at least five years.

- With the number of electric razors the company sells in a year, it can't afford to hire a famous spokesperson to promote sales.
- By far the most important distribution channel for women's electric razors is department stores.

An idea inspired by questioning these assumptions could be: What if the company marketed an inexpensive "bikini" electric razor, targeted toward teenage girls, coming in a range of exciting colors and designs, endorsed by a young, up-and-coming movie star, selling for $14.95 in drugstores, merchandised next to the suntan lotion, and available in warm-weather months? An idea like a teenage-girl's electric bikini shaver makes it easy to see the power of this technique. It not only challenges the assumptions a company might make about the kinds of products it offers, but also how it positions, markets, prices, merchandises, and distributes these products.

opportunity redefinition

My first book had just come out, and I got a call from the Catholic Knights Insurance Company in Milwaukee, Wisconsin. If you've never heard of the Catholic Knights Insurance Company, you're not alone. I hadn't either. It sells insurance only to Catholics, a clause written in its charter, and this (they would say inclusionary) policy has been successfully defended in court.

The company, through the leadership of its enlightened CEO, Dan Steininger, had pursued a companywide quality initiative with both extraordinary passion and superior results. It became nationally recognized as a best-in-class quality practitioner.

And then, to the CEO's credit, he asked, "What's next?" He felt they had done all they could in getting their systems right and building an environment that championed both individual initiative and team cooperation. His conclusion (helped in part by reading my first book, he told me) was that the next "next" was creativity. So he invited me to Milwaukee, where I spent a couple of days working with a cross-functional team of managers, salespeople, and customer service representatives. It was an extraordinary experience and a lot of fun.

As part of their quality program, the CEO had encouraged lunch-time book discussion clubs. Everyone in the company was given a copy of my book and asked to read it and then discuss it. Consequently they knew the book well. And so I was barraged with a variety of interesting and insightful questions about creative principles and stories I had written about in the book.

There is a paradox in the world of consulting. Common sense would tell you that the companies that need your consulting expertise most would be the ones that were most likely to benefit from your experience and counsel and, conversely, that the companies that are already world class would benefit the least. My experience has shown me that exactly the opposite is true. It is only the really great client that can accept great help. Catholic Knights Insurance, it turns out, was a great client.

Based on presession discussions with their senior leaders, we decided to focus the ideation session on helping them grow their business. Specifically, we were looking for ways to increase sales of life insurance to Catholics. I trained the workshop participants in a number of techniques, all successful, all very much appreciated, but one technique was directly responsible for a multimillion-dollar increase in sales. The technique is called opportunity redefinition, and as you will see, its use has applications well beyond increasing sales.

To try the opportunity redefinition technique, you start with an opportunity statement, or creative challenge. Ours was very simple: "How do we sell more insurance to Catholics?" Can't get much more straightforward than that.

Next comes the redefinition. To redefine the opportunity, pick three of the more interesting words in the sentence and generate eight to ten creative alternatives for each choice. You might think of choosing words that represent a who, what, when, where, or how. The three words we chose were, "How do *we sell* more insurance to *Catholics*?" For the first word, *we,* our team generated a list of ten creative alternatives for who else the "we" could be—for example:

- The sales force
- The clergy
- Friends of Catholics
- Churchgoers
- Catholic family members
- Catholic Knights (CK) board members
- CK customer service reps
- Sales force relatives
- CK's PR department
- Policyholders

We then generated a list of ten creative alternatives for each of the other two selected words: *sell* and *Catholics*, and placed all three sets of creative alternatives under the original opportunity challenge: How do *we sell* more insurance to *Catholics*?

we	sell	Catholics
sales force	license	Catholic doctors
the clergy	give away	Catholic athletes
friends of Catholics	test-run	Catholic students
churchgoers	comarket	Catholic donators
Catholic family members	promote	Catholic schools
CK board members	advertise	Catholic dioceses
CK customer service	telemarket	Catholic summer camps
sales force relatives	network	Catholic grandparents
CK's PR department	be incentivized	the Vatican
policyholders	reward	Catholic evangelists

Then the fun started. We started redefining the opportunity by randomly combining words from each of the three to give us an entirely new opportunity statement. Here are a few examples:

1. How do we get *friends of Catholics* to *be incentivized* to sell life insurance to *Catholic grandparents*?

2. How do we get *Catholic Knight board members* to *license* the selling
    of life insurance to *Catholic schools*?
3. How do we get *policyholders* to *be rewarded* for selling more life
    insurance at [or to] *the Vatican*?

These crazy combination sentences are then used as starting points
or brainstorming triggers to generate new selling ideas. So, for instance,
in opportunity restatement 1, it could be taken literally. Maybe you
really could figure out a way to incentivize friends of Catholics to sell
life insurance to Catholic grandparents: "Could you create a sales force
of retirees [friends of Catholics] to network and sell life insurance to
Catholic grandparents?"

More likely though, you'll want to take the statement less literally
and use it simply as a jumping-off point for the team's brainstorming.
It might inspire an idea such as: "A program to incentivize grandparents to give life insurance policies to their children for the sake of their
grandchildren."

Now look at restatement 2, "How do we get *Catholic Knight board
members* to *license* the selling of life insurance to *Catholic schools*?"
How about if you created a program where Catholic Knights Insurance gave much-needed athletic equipment to Catholic schools for
every X number of parents of that school's children who took
out policies?"

Then go to restatement 3: "How do we get *policyholders* to be
rewarded for selling more life insurance at [or to] *the Vatican*?" How
about a contest where policyholders could win a trip for themselves
and their family to the Vatican (and possibly meet the pope) just for
sitting through a Catholic Knight's sales presentation?" And so on. I
don't think it's at all a stretch to imagine that by using this technique,
you could immediately start generating creative selling ideas and sales
strategies even when you're operating under so potentially limiting a
constraint as having to sell life insurance only to Catholics.

Consider how many possible opportunity redefinitions you would
have in the above example: 10 × 10 × 10, or 1,000 possible redefinitions.

Of course, many (or most) of these redefinitions may not get you any new or exciting ideas, but some certainly will. And you need only a few big ideas—or maybe even just one—to see a dramatic impact on your business.

In the case of Catholic Knights, because of their background and training in Total Quality Management and its accompanying metrics, they were accustomed to being very conscientious about their work. Consequently, they were extremely rigorous in the application of this technique, generating literally hundreds of redefined opportunity statements, which ultimately led to dozens of new creative sales strategies and ideas. What were the actual results? The vice president of sales sent me a letter verifying that this technique alone led to a 52 percent increase in sales.

Beyond increasing sales, how else might you use this technique? In the broadest sense, anything you can put into a sentence could be an opportunity to be redefined. I have found the technique particularly useful with seemingly impossible challenges. Interestingly, it's through the use of this technique that you'll often discover that the challenge only seems impossible because, as I sometimes say, the tyranny of words has imposed their inherent limitations on the infinite possibilities of creative thought. Ironically, of course, this technique essentially uses words to go beyond the limitations of words.

A few words, then, from a master of words, playwright Arthur Miller: "The job is to ask questions—it always was—and to ask them as *inexorably* as I can." Could we say the same of a facilitating leader? If we can, doesn't it make sense for that person to be proactive in the creation of questions as a way to grow and improve the business? And could the opportunity redefinition technique, simple as it is, help generate those questions without the manager's having to invest too much time or effort? And finally, can you imagine what it might be like to work for someone who, every day, as inexorably as he could, asked you questions designed to help liberate your true creative potential?

wishing

Wishing literally changed my life. I had just graduated from college, and it was my use of wishing (the wishing technique, that is) that helped me get a job in advertising—though I didn't yet know such an ideation technique existed. And I got the job during a very tough recession, when seemingly no one was hiring anyone, especially a kid fresh out of college with no experience.

Wishing is another technique that works well in apparently impossible situations. My "impossible" wish was to meet and interview with the top ad agency presidents in New York City, since my first six months of job hunting had convinced me that interviewing with human resources wasn't going to get me anywhere. My wish also included meeting these presidents right away, since I was still living at home and desperately felt I needed to get on with my life and career.

This wish inspired me to create a promotional event I called "Jogging for Jobs." I placed an ad in the *New York Times* asking other ad agency hopefuls who were recent graduates to join me in a job-hunting jog to drop off our résumés at the city's largest agencies. My hope was that if I could get enough publicity for the event, the agency presidents might be willing to meet our intrepid group of Manhattan Island joggers.

And so, over three magical and fun days, the "Go-Getters," as I had called us in the press releases, jogged to the top thirty-six New York ad agencies. Because it was timely, fun, and unique, it became a successful publicity stunt that was covered in the advertising column of the *New York Times* (twice), over the AP wire service, on New York's *Eyewitness News,* and on CBS Radio. Ultimately we joggers met with twenty-four of the thirty-six presidents of New York's top ad agencies. And all of us who jogged for the entire three days of the event got jobs.

Ever since Jogging for Jobs, I have been a big believer in the power of wishing.

The wishing technique is simple. You start by wishing for the impossible and then figure out a way to make the impossible, or at least some approximation of the impossible, a reality. As futurist and *2001: A Space Odyssey* author Arthur C. Clarke was fond of saying, "We cannot know what's possible without first considering the impossible." So it is with wishing. The wishing technique begins with the assumption that anything is possible. Money, energy, and time are no object. You can even violate laws of nature. If you can dare to imagine it, you can have it with wishing. And because anything is possible in the world of wishing, going there helps a person or a team challenge perceived limitations around any creative challenge or opportunity.

The wishing technique is facilitated much like the questioning assumptions technique, in two steps:

Step 1: The facilitating leader has the team generate twenty to thirty wishes.

Step 2: The team works through several of the more fantastic or impossible wishes and uses them as creative stimuli to generate novel but realistic ideas.

A good example of wishing in action came when I was demonstrating the technique for a group of high-potential managers with the City of New York. I had asked for a particularly thorny challenge the city was facing, and one of the managers suggested traffic congestion.

So we started wishing, close in at first:

"I wish there were fewer cabs."
"I wish we had a big circle of commuter parking lots all around the city so no one would have to drive their cars into midtown."
"I wish trucks could come in only at night to the city."

Then with my prompting, we began to wish much further out, even though such fantastical wishing can be a real challenge for adults:

"I wish cars could stand on their tailpipes, so you could park more cars on the street."

"I wish you could compress a car to the size of a key so you could hold it in your hand."

"I wish cars could float. Have an antigravity button, so you could park cars in the sky."

I next asked the participants to start wishing specifically from the perspective of a driver stuck in traffic congestion in New York City:

"I wish I knew the best and easiest route to take given today's traffic."

"I wish I was telepathic and knew which street had open parking spaces."

"I wish I could make other cars disappear."

We ended step 1 with twenty wishes. In step 2, we worked several of these wishes to see if they might inspire a new idea. The telepathy wish, for example, led the group to a simple idea that we thought had potential for reducing traffic congestion. Some hotels use a signal light to tell cabbies that a hotel guest needs a ride. What if the city installed lights at the end of every street block to signal if there was an open parking space? (Relatively low-cost laser monitors could be attached to parking meters to signal which spaces were open on a particular street.) The system could potentially reduce traffic congestion by making it much more efficient to find an open parking space. Drivers would not continually be cruising the streets looking for an open space.

As a prompt halfway through the first step of the exercise, I had the participants adopt the role of a driver caught in traffic and wish from her perspective. We call this *role-play wishing* or *target market wishing,* and it's a way to help focus the wish technique while still promoting imaginative thinking. A good example of using role-play wishing was in a new product development project we did for the Danaher Tool Group, at the time part of Danaher Corporation, the highly profitable Fortune 200 company that made select Craftsman tools for Sears. Our assignment was to help them invent new ratchet, wrench, and socket sets. Our research had shown that although it was already a huge business, there was still an opportunity for growth by providing specialized sets for different target markets. And so we had the ideation team role-play different target markets and make imaginative wishes about how a new set could be designed and packaged to meet each target market's specialized needs. Over half a dozen successful new ratchet, wrench, and socket sets came out of this work, including sets for motorcycle, truck, and boat owners, as well as gift givers and do-it-yourself women.

triggered brainwalking

More than any other ideation technique, brainwalking lends itself to being combined with other techniques.[1] Brainwalking is a great way to ensure that everyone gets a chance to contribute ideas. The kinds of ideas, in terms of both number and quality, can be dramatically improved in brainwalking by triggering these rotations with other thought-provoking techniques. Consequently, we have triggered brainwalking with literally dozens of other techniques, sometimes using as many as three or four techniques in one brainwalk exercise. For instance, in a recent ideation session for a new lipstick product, we triggered the brainwalk with four prompts, in the following order:

1. Target market wishes
2. Category reframes and redefinitions: lip reshaping, lip recontouring, lip sculpting, lip firming, and lip highlighting, for example
3. Benefit-oriented trigger words: *continuous moisturization, dimensionalized color, lip massaging, freshening, multiple-use, energizing,* and so on
4. The worst idea technique

Think of the brainwalking technique as vanilla ice cream. Yes, it's by far the most popular flavor of ice cream and delicious all by itself, but start adding things to it—bananas, chocolate sauce, walnuts, sprinkles, and whipped cream—and you've got something very special.

semantic intuition

The creative word combination technique known as semantic intuition was invented in 1972 by Helmut Schlicksupp, an employee of Battelle's German office. It's one of my favorite new product development techniques because:

- It always works.
- It's both energizing and a lot of fun to do, especially when ideators are starting to feel brain-dead toward the end of an ideation session.
- It inspires different ideas from other techniques, often extremely practical or immediately doable ideas.
- It's a good example of a technique that has to be creatively customized to reach its full effectiveness.

Semantic intuition prompts participants to create new ideas by having them combine several categories of key words to create a name for a new idea—and this is before they have any concept of what this newly named idea is. As counterintuitive as it may seem, naming an idea before knowing what it could be is indeed how the technique works. (I've included a detailed explanation of the technique in Chapter Nine, including the rationale for using it specifically for new product ideation.) Let's see how this technique might play out if it were to be used to create a new retail promotion idea for a common household product, a detergent.

To name our new idea, we'll first need three related categories of words (these ultimately will be randomly combined to create the names). To inspire retail and store promotions for a detergent, we might consider using the following three categories of words: (1) places in a store, (2) kinds of promotional appeals, and (3) benefits of the product or general interests of the target market consumer.

The lists of words for places in the store might include *aisles, parking lot, frozen section, bakery, photo department, customer service, pharmacy,* and *flower shop.* Examples of kinds of promotional appeals could be: Buy One Get One, Shelf Talkers, Gift with Purchase, Instantly Redeemable Coupon, floor stands and displays, and at-register coupons.

And product benefits or interests of the target market might include product benefits like clean clothes, getting stains out, and fresh-smelling clothes, or target market interests like baseball games, family dinners, and a trip to Disney World.

Next, the words are randomly combined, one from each category or list of words, to create the name for a new idea. For example, one name (or, if you prefer, thought starter) combination might be: "photo department, gift with purchase, and clean clothes." This admittedly odd combination might inspire you and another team member to create an idea like this one:

> You'd have before-and-after, point-of-sale materials/posters in the photo department of the retail store. The Before Pictures (before using the detergent, of course), and the after pictures (after using the detergent) could accomplish two things. The photos/posters could be fun/entertaining/adorable before-and-after pictures of dirty and then clean kids, thus promoting the cleaning power of the specific detergent, while reinforcing positive associations for the brand. But even more important for the retailer, these photos/posters could be a cost-free way (since the manufacturer would pay for them) for the store to promote its high-margin photo-processing department.

Your first reaction to this idea might be, "How did you get such a well-thought-out idea just from the 'photo department, gift with purchase, and clean clothes' prompt? And that was without even using the 'gift with purchase' phrase in the concept." You're right to ask this question. These word combination thought starters are just that: thought starters for creative thinking. You have permission (and indeed should encourage everyone using this technique) to go beyond the literal meaning of the words to create a workable idea. The combinations are simply stimuli to prompt you to think differently. Nor should you feel obligated to use all three words to help you get an idea. If you use only two of the words (as I did in the example) or even none of the words, it doesn't matter. The point is that you're looking for new, original ideas. How you get to these ideas is not important.

picture prompts

We were working with a large cheese company. One of its senior marketing executives (we'll call him Bob) came to me and asked if I might help him with a business management problem. He was feeling overworked and stressed. To his credit, he'd figured out the cause of his problem: he had trouble delegating. He was micromanaging and consequently working much harder than he needed to or should. He knew something had to give.

I scheduled Bob's issue into a creativity training session I was running for a group of other executives from other companies with whom he met monthly to discuss and brainstorm business issues. I used the creative technique picture prompts to problem-solve his management challenge. The reason I chose this is that visual techniques have a way of bringing to the surface intuitions, emotions, and feelings. So it's a good technique for personnel and management creative challenges, which can often have an emotional or psychological root cause. Picture prompts is also a quick exercise. The facilitating leader simply passes out preselected visuals and asks session participants for new ideas somehow inspired by what they are seeing in the visuals. It's straightforward with intentionally simple instructions—for example, "Does this picture help you think of any ideas that could help solve the problem?" The visuals I used for this exercise, from my ten-year collection of award-winning illustrations from *Communication Arts* and other design magazines, were preselected for:

- Variety of subject matter
- Visual interest

- Depiction of people in all kinds of interactions and relationships with other people

I framed the creative challenge this way: "How can we help Bob delegate better?" and passed out the three pictures to each of the session's twelve participants. "Imagine that the answer to his problem is contained in one of the pictures I just passed out to you," I said. "See if you can find it." I next said, "Now that you've looked at your pictures, I'd like you to share with a partner what you saw and thought from your pictures. Then see, if together, the two of you can come up with an idea or two that will help Bob delegate better."

The teams of two then presented their ideas. The idea that the group was most excited about came from two senior executives who had a Magritte-style painting, where two bowler-hatted, proper gentlemen were facing each other while simultaneously handing each other a letter. It was this cooperative handing off of the letters that gave them their idea. Typically delegation of work is a one-way, top-down, semi-dictatorial act. There's nothing particularly cooperative about it.

So they asked, "Could the delegation of work somehow be made more cooperative?" Instead of Bob deciding who would be delegated what, why couldn't his direct reports work with Bob to choose what they were most interested in doing from Bob's list of tasks for delegation?

There were several advantages to this approach. For one, it would ensure that the tasks that were being delegated had someone assigned to them who was passionate and committed to succeed with the assignment. Since they chose it, they would feel increased internal and external pressure to bring it to a successful conclusion, even if they didn't quite yet have the necessary skills to pull it off. Second, it gave Bob a chance to get to know his people better; it brought to the surface their unique interests, loves, and thinking styles. This knowledge, above and beyond delegating tasks, could help make him a better manager. Finally, the whole process of cooperative delegation, as we called it, made Bob feel more like a coworker and friend than someone's boss.

Bob wouldn't admit it, but I suspected that this was part of his reticence to assign tasks in the old command-and-control model of delegation.

One of the advantages of the picture prompts technique is that you can customize the visuals to address a particular kind of creative challenge. If you have a management issue, as I did with Bob, select visuals that portray people in a variety of interesting situations. If you're working on a manufacturing problem, select pictures of industrial scenes, as well as things being made, manipulated, or transformed. If you're working on new products, select pictures that might relate to your product category: outdoor scenes for outdoor sports equipment or food or food ingredient visuals for new snack ideas, for example. Of course, you'll also want to include a certain percentage of purely random visuals in your exercise as well. Remember the fourth creative mind-set from Chapter One, principle finding and principle transfer: the human mind has an uncanny ability to make creative connections between seemingly random or irrelevant stimuli.

worst idea

I was dying up there. Forty minutes into a three-hour workshop for over seventy-five bankers on how to inject creativity into their marketing, and nothing—I mean NOTHING—was working. It was uncomfortable for me and, I suspect, for my audience as well. Then I decided I would demonstrate, with their help, the worst idea technique. I'm pretty sure I was thinking, *Well, I can't do any worse than this, so let's go all the way and do the worst idea technique.*

This technique is very simple. You first get the participants to collectively create a list of bad ideas. Really terrible ideas. Awful ideas. Stupid ideas. Illegal ideas. Gross ideas. Then you have the participants work to turn these worst ideas into good ideas by either having them think of the opposite of the worst idea or, as bad as the idea is, find something of interest or value in the bad idea to inspire a good idea.

For these bankers, I introduced the worst idea technique by saying "I'd like you to come up not with *good* ideas for marketing your bank and its financial products, but with the worst ideas you can think of. These ideas could be stupid, crazy, gross, or even illegal. Have fun! Break the rules. I'm not kidding. I really want you to push yourself to come up with really bad ideas."

Uncapped marker in hand, a blank page of flip chart paper, I was ready to write down their terrible ideas.

Still nothing. Blank stares. Finally, thank goodness, one of the bank marketers said something.

"Well, we could close the bank at noon instead of 3:00."

Everyone laughed. Banker humor, I guess.

Followed by, "We could double the ATM fees!"

More laughter.

"That's not bad enough," I said. "I want even worse ideas!"

"Well, we could have the ATMs intentionally break down every time someone tried to get money out. Then we'd keep more money in deposits."

"You're getting better—or is it worse?" I said.

"Here's a really bad idea. We could round down everyone's deposits to the nearest dollar. Most people probably wouldn't notice."

"No, we'll make a mistake in their favor, give everyone extra money every time they make a transaction. Now that's a bad idea!"

More laughter, even louder.

The worst idea technique saved the day. The workshop took off, and great energy and great ideas flowed effortlessly. It was a lot of fun, too.

The worst idea technique seems like a frivolous exercise, but it's not. Having gone back and analyzed the output of a number of ideation sessions for both quality and quantity of ideas, I can confirm that the worst idea technique is one of the most productive, especially in terms of quality (as determined by the session participants' votes for "the best ideas"). I believe there are several reasons that the worst idea technique works so well. For one, probably more than any other technique, it takes the creative pressure off. It allows people to relax and have fun. Participants may not be sure they can come up with a good idea, but they certainly know that they can come up with a bad one.

And even when the facilitating leader says, "Hey, that idea's not bad enough!" as I did with the bank marketers, no one ever takes offense. They know it's a good-natured prompt, to help everyone have more fun and laugh!

And of course laughter also helps explain the success of this technique. Laughing loosens up people, making it more likely that they will come up with surprising or unexpected connections. Finally, I think the worst idea technique is so productive because it's hard to think of a bad idea without then also considering its opposite, or positive cousin: a good idea.

After the group generates a list of bad ideas, the team uses them to inspire a good idea. For example, the worst idea of "We could round down everyone's deposits to the nearest dollar" is very close to the Keep the Change savings program that Bank of America launched a number of years ago, except that depositors get to keep the money from their "rounded-down" checking account. Another example of the effectiveness of the worst idea was when we used it in a new product development session for one of our information services clients. After triggering the brainwalk technique with a series of target market wishes, we did a rotation in the brainwalk that included the worst idea technique.

Given the company's business model, compiling and selling information, the worst possible idea becomes obvious very quickly: instead of charging for information, give it away. At first blush, this would certainly be a formula for disaster. But as the team explored this worst of all worst ideas and tried to find at least something of value in it, they realized that it could indeed contain the seed of an interesting idea. No, they wouldn't give away all their data. But could they give away a small portion of their data as a marketing tool and as a way to add to the richness and robustness of their current database? They could and they did. This worst idea–inspired idea ultimately became a multimillion-dollar revenue generator.

■ ■ ■

Now that you have a tool kit of focused ideation techniques, what's next for a great facilitating leader? Well, conceiving a great idea is only half the battle. (And some might say "half the battle" is overstating it.) For many, the bigger challenge is getting that idea successfully to market. Innovating ideas often takes more creativity and creative leadership than conceiving an idea. In the next chapters, we turn to some of the most critical innovation skills facilitating leaders are likely to need to bring an idea successfully to market.

4

innovation overview
strategies and tools of a successful innovation process

Prospective clients sometimes say to me, "Our problem isn't ideas. We have plenty of ideas. The real challenge is getting these ideas to market successfully." This is, of course, what innovation is all about. And typically companies stumble at this getting-ideas-to-market phase, though not for lack of a process. Most companies already have a perfectly reasonable new product development (or stage-gating) process. They fail because they don't have the necessary talent, resources, experience, or corporate commitment to develop their ideas successfully within their existing process. Put another way, bringing innovations to market successfully is less about analyzing an idea's market potential (although this is certainly important). Rather, it is, above all, about getting the consumer proposition correct. And getting this proposition correct (including its price-to-value equation; the product's positioning; and how it's packaged, distributed, and displayed) takes every bit as much creativity, at every stage of the idea's development, as it did to conceive of the idea.

This chapter contains three process suggestions to help you get your consumer proposition correct: idea fishing, opportunity area platform creation, and iterative insight mining. Applied conscientiously and rigorously, they should lead to improved success rates for your new product initiatives. Indeed, for my company's packaged goods consulting clients, we have new product success rates upward of 70 percent versus industry averages of only 10 to 20 percent. Also, it's important to note that all of the innovation process suggestions that follow can be easily adapted to or incorporated into existing new product development processes.

I'll cover the three process suggestions shortly, but we first need to be clear about the kinds of ideas you, your team, and your company are looking for.

looking for disruptive innovations?

The term *disruptive innovation* was coined by Clayton Christensen[1] of the Harvard Business School. Simply put, disruptive innovations can literally disrupt, or even totally redefine and reinvent, an established category of products or services. Typically, disruptive innovations provide new consumer or customer benefits that are often delivered in totally new or unexpected ways. Examples of disruptive innovations are digital photography, which made film photography obsolete; MRIs as an alternative to X-rays; digital calculators, which replaced slide rules; and downloading books on the Kindle or Nook instead of buying printed books.

Typically the term *disruptive innovation* is associated with disrupting competitive categories and markets into which the innovation is introduced. Interestingly, we've found in our innovation consulting work that truly disruptive innovations can be as disruptive to the established innovation structures and processes inside an organization as they are to the categories outside the organization that they are designed to revolutionize.

In theory, being disruptively innovative makes a great deal of business sense: the chance to own a high-margin monopoly, at least for a period of time, in a newly created category is attractive indeed. The reality, though, is that it is extremely tough to both invent and successfully market a disruptive innovation: it's risky and time-consuming; it typically requires large investments of development capital and employee resources; and it is tremendously challenging to bring all the elements of a new product or service together in an integrated and compelling way. Some of our clients have asked us, at least initially, to help them create disruptive innovations. But as we worked our disruptive innovative process, we discovered that they really wanted less-than-truly-disruptive innovations—in other words, innovative new products or services that could help them make their yearly sales number. Specifically, this meant they were looking for new products that could be manufactured on their current lines (or easily outsourced), leverage the equity in their current brands or trademarks, be sold by their current sales force to their traditional retail accounts and buyers, and be distributed through the company's current distribution system (warehousing or direct store delivery).

Are less disruptive innovations easier to market? They certainly are, since you don't have to create a new brand, sell to a new buyer, market through a different channel, or, as in some truly disruptive innovations, invent a new distribution channel.

Are less disruptive innovations easier to create than disruptive innovations? Not necessarily. With a disruptive innovation, you have the creative freedom to dream without limitations or constraints. With less disruptive innovations, you have a host of "guardrails" that limit the kinds and numbers of ideas that the company is willing to pursue.

Discovering and fulfilling an unmet need in an established category is very difficult, even if you're clever enough in your innovation approach to begin by redefining that established category, because your competition generally is trying every bit as hard as you are to find "the next big thing." Consider also that in an established category, you're more likely to have well-funded, entrenched competition that's highly motivated to aggressively defend its share of market in the current category.

So what do you do if, like most companies, the reality is that you are more interested in creating less disruptive innovations than trying to create truly disruptive ones? We have found that the innovation process that works for clients looking for disruptive innovations works equally well for clients interested in creating less disruptive innovation. This process can be thought of in three phases: idea fishing, creating opportunity area platforms, and evolving ideas into motivating consumer propositions in a process we call iterative insight mining.

idea fishing: the how, where, and what of innovation idea gathering and creation

Your company may already have more ideas than it knows what to do with, but the critical question really is, "How good are these ideas?" and maybe even more to the point, "How can you evolve these good ideas [assuming you even know which ideas are the good ones] into great ideas?"

What follows are sixteen categories of approaches, thinking strategies, and research methodologies that my company uses to generate and evolve nascent ideas into great new products, new services, and new businesses that have a greater chance of succeeding in the marketplace. Think of these approaches and strategies as knowing how and where to fish for new ideas.

#1 Consumer Insights

My partner and I believe strongly that innovation begins and ends with the consumer. So working to find consumer (or customer) insights to both inspire new innovations and further develop and refine ideas we already have is key. We use seven consumer insight approaches:

- *Conventional focus groups:* Conducting research in a focus group facility with a variety of target market consumers, including placing samples of new products in the consumers' homes before they arrive at the focus group session
- *Ethnographic approaches:* Conducting interviews in the home or in places where a consumer would actually use the potential new product; for example, talking with men about a new car wax as they wash and wax their car in their driveway
- *Online focus groups:* Using online video technology to interact with consumers (usually three simultaneously) no matter where they live
- *Shopper intercepts/shop-alongs:* Interviewing and accompanying shoppers to specific retail outlets as they shop in that store's departments and aisles
- *Quantitative research:* Using the results of large market studies with hundreds or even thousands of consumers to help identify unmet needs and opportunities for new products in a particular product category; often reserved for assessing the market potential of well-developed concepts
- *Supplier's consumer panels:* Sometimes used by fragrance houses and other ingredient suppliers that are willing to do consumer research, free of charge, in the hopes of helping to create a market for a new ingredient
- *Customer service call centers:* Mining the data from a company's call center, which can lead to product improvement ideas, as well as entirely new lines of products

All of these research methodologies enable us and our clients to uncover new insights and ideas we would be unlikely to discover any other way, including discerning good ideas from not-so-good ideas. Good ideas can become great ideas by refining and tweaking the elements of the new product mix until there is an integrated and winning new product proposition.

#2 Supplier Outreach and Consulting

Suppliers can be a great source of new ideas. In the world of new product development, companies that do subcontracted manufacturing often have proprietary manufacturing machines, processes, and expertise that can, with a little creativity, inspire new product concepts with different forms, ingredients, and, presumably, different consumer benefits. And in most cases, these contract manufacturers, or copackers, are only too willing to have you and your innovation team work with them to learn the capabilities of their manufacturing plants. They know that helping you could lead to a new idea product that could be subcontract manufactured at their plant. Suppliers are also often willing to send their manufacturing and process engineers, free of charge, to participate in your internal ideation sessions.

Manufacturers are not the only kinds of suppliers that can help. We have used five other types of suppliers to help us in our innovation consulting work:

- Suppliers to suppliers—for instance, those that supply the raw materials to your manufacturing partner
- Academia and other associations, including research labs conducting both theoretical and applied materials research; MIT's Media Lab is a good example of both
- Market research partners, including social media monitoring organizations
- Agencies: advertising, promotion, public relations, digital, and so on
- Freelancers and consultants: marketing, supply chain, trade representatives, and so on

We have found, for instance, that effectively leveraging the knowledge and expertise of market research partners such as Symphony IRI, TNS, and Ipsos can be a tremendous asset in helping to identify new consumer insights and specific opportunity areas for new product ideation.

Most Fortune 500 companies, especially packaged-goods manufacturers, have contracts with social media monitoring organizations like NetBase or ListenLogic to monitor and assess what everyday consumers are saying about their company, their brands, and their products. Companies that are not willing to pay a subscription fee for a social media monitoring service can use free Web-searching services such as Social Mention or Topsy. From an innovation standpoint, these social media monitoring organizations can be an important source of consumer dissatisfactions, wishes, or unmet needs in a particular category and therefore help inspire new product ideas, innovative marketing programs, or promotions.

#3 Employee Outreach

Making companywide suggestion box programs work is often a challenge because they require a tremendous commitment in company time and resources. However, there are easier, quicker, and more cost-effective ways to creatively involve employees in the innovation process. In addition to the whiteboard technique (see Chapter Five), we have seen three other approaches work well:

- Invention, problem-solving, and naming competitions
- R&D innovation fairs
- Employees as research subjects

To get a quick and cost-effective read on new product concepts, we often do taste tests with employees and their families. One of our client's suppliers once helped us out by taste-testing several of our new product concepts at their annual company picnic.

We've also seen invention, problem-solving, and naming competitions work. Unlike a general suggestion box, they are a creative challenge with specific creative parameters and goals, with defined start and end dates.

An R&D innovation fair is a fun and effective way to highlight some of the further out, even potentially less practical ideas that

R&D might be working on. Typically R&D will set up a conference room at corporate headquarters and fill it with their new product ideas and concepts. Company employees are invited to tour the new product exhibits, fill out evaluation forms, and even make suggestions for improvement. Often the R&D prototypes spark interesting questions, insights, product names, and other idea builds that can add energy and excitement to the prototype concepts. It's a wonderful way for non-R&D employees to be a part of the idea creation and process, while providing R&D with valuable consumer input at no charge to the company.

#4 Inventive Crowdsourcing

A number of firms have emerged that act as an innovation and problem-solving conduit between internal R&D departments and outside inventors and technical specialists. Procter & Gamble, for which we have done a number of new product development projects, has been a pioneer in using these firms to help leverage technical specialists, many from academic research labs, to solve seemingly intractable technical challenges quickly and cost-effectively.

Crowdsourcing services and contests have also been used to create thirty-second commercials, name new products, and design logos. An innovation friend and colleague, Matt Greeley, president of the company Bright Ideas, has created the online software that helps inventors submit new ideas to companies. GE, for instance, has used Bright Idea's software to create a successful crowdsourcing program, "Ecomagination Challenge, Powering Your Home." GE was looking for inventions to help it exploit what has become known as the "smart grid": data on the generation and distribution of energy. Of the 856 idea submissions to the Ecomagination Challenge, the GE Energy team selected five winners. Each received a prize of $100,000. One of the winning inventions, PlotWatt, for instance, allows homeowners to know exactly how much energy each appliance in their home is using.

As crowdsourcing methodologies continue to evolve, with increasing numbers of companies acting as intermediaries between organizations and crowds of individuals hoping to make a creative contribution to that organization, one can only imagine the potential for improving both the number and quality of corporate innovations.

#5 Internal Research and the Innovation Audit

When we begin working with a client on an innovation project, we are often amazed at how much research a company has already done that can be leveraged for new insights and innovation opportunities. Increasingly, we are hearing clients say that they are concerned that they are not devoting sufficient time to mining the research for insights, especially since the market research typically costs millions of dollars annually. We discover innovation opportunities from existing, in-house research and knowledge in four ways:

- *An innovation audit*—one-on-one opportunity interviews with scientists and researchers from both the R&D and market research departments
- *Mining market studies and segmentation research* to identify unmet needs and opportunities in the specific categories of products
- *Reviewing other consumer research*, primarily for insights into consumer attitudes, behaviors, and preferences
- *Reviewing the results of previously tested concepts*, which may have scored well but were never developed further or may not have tested well, but because of changing market conditions or a new consumer insight could be resurrected into a new product success

An innovation audit reveals at least four kinds of existing ideas or projects: (1) ideas that were not of sufficient interest to pursue further at the time, (2) ideas launched in the marketplace that failed, (3) ideas that were put on hold because they couldn't be manufactured at the right price or value, or needed an as-yet-unknown technological advance to be viable, or (4) ideas that never got sufficient internal support to merit further development.

A good example of waiting for a technological advance was work we did some time ago for Centrum Silver. The ideation session with internal employees, and follow-up qualitative research with men fifty years old or above, made abundantly clear the need for a specialized line of vitamins that could promote heart health. At the time, there was no natural, vitamin-appropriate, and stable ingredient that could do this. It wasn't until the development of the ingredient CoroWise, which has phytosterols to help reduce cholesterol in the blood, that the Centrum Specialist product for the heart became viable.

An example of a product that failed the first time around but has now been reintroduced successfully is Thomas' Corn English Muffin. We knew from our initial home-use-test focus group research for Thomas' that the idea of a corn english muffin was very attractive to a wide variety of consumers, especially Hispanic consumers who particularly liked the taste of a sweeter English muffin. The challenge was that we could never get the product that was manufactured on the line to taste as good as the lab samples we were testing in the focus groups. As a result, the product that was launched into the market the first time failed. Four years later, these technical manufacturing challenges had been solved. The relaunched product now tastes wonderful and is doing well in the marketplace.

Regarding the other three research areas of opportunity (mining market studies and segmentation research, reviewing other consumer research, and reviewing the results of previously tested concepts), we have found that one of the best ways to exploit these existing resources for new ideas is to use them as the basis for a half-day or even a full-day ideation session. The ideation session has the ability to transform hard-to-read or confusing data into compelling innovation strategies.

A case in point was an ideation session we conducted for one of the large bottled water companies, which owned more than a half-dozen regional and national bottled water brands. Their market research and consumer segmentation study revealed five very different consumer segments buying bottled water. To make the consumer segmentation research come alive, we had the group do a series of consumer role plays, with different teams playing different target market consumers. The role plays made it easy for everyone in the room to understand exactly who these different consumers were and what specifically they were looking for in bottled water: price, convenience, added flavor, the water source or processing method, brand prestige and heritage, and others. After the role play, the group built sales and marketing strategies for each of the different brands of bottled water in the company's portfolio based on the needs and wants of the uniquely different consumer segments. It was a fun and creative way to build an integrated growth strategy for all of the brands in the company's portfolio, with each element of the strategy informed by the market research.

#6 Internal "Joint Ventures"
Typically a joint venture involves partnering with companies outside yours. These could be noncompeting manufacturers; local, regional, national, or international brands that could be comarketed with or complement your product or brand (think of a pack of Mars' M&Ms inside Kraft's Lunchables); companies with alternative distribution systems or models; or even venture capitalists. But sometimes "internal joint ventures"—working with other R&D groups in the company; ideating comarketing opportunities with other company-owned brands; or even being creative about how to leverage share or different distribution channels across brands—can be as exciting and productive as external joint ventures. For example, before Kraft split into two companies, Kraft and Mondelez, it owned Trident and Tang, both billion-dollar brands worldwide. An obvious idea would have been for Trident to offer a Tang-flavored gum.

Another internal venture idea is to generate cross-selling opportunities between divisions. For the financial services company Fiserv, for instance, we created and facilitated a day-long ideation to identify cross-selling opportunities across eight of their different companies or divisions. The result (valued by the sales executives in the session) was over $125 million in new selling opportunities, $72 million of which was realized in less than a year.

It's interesting, and somewhat counterintuitive, that because of internal politics, you may find it harder to pull off an internal joint venture than an external one. Our experience at Growth Engine is that a particularly good time to do one of these joint internal venture ideation sessions is soon after one company acquires another: typically there will be an openness to working together and jointly creating new products and services that might not exist in the future when each company begins to return to its traditional ways of doing business.

#7 Licensing

We think of licensing in two ways: (1) products, technologies, or brands that could be "in-licensed" to complement a company's current intellectual property or (2) products, technologies, or brands owned by the company that could be out-licensed, to create additional streams of revenue. Even if you and your team have no plans to in-license other brands or out-license your current brands, it can be a valuable creative exercise to imagine what brands could complement yours and potentially bring you into entirely new product categories and other categories of products or services where you can leverage your brands' current equities.

Designing and facilitating ideation sessions for a leading licensing firm, Leveraged Marketing Corporation of America (LMCA), taught me that it's not always obvious how far you can extend your brand. For instance, one of LMCA's most successful licenses is with Kodak; it has licensed the Kodak name for high-quality eyeglass lenses. It was not an obvious idea initially, but in retrospect, it was a brilliant one since it leveraged Kodak's heritage and reputation as an expert in visual media.

A more obvious idea that came out of a licensing ideation session we facilitated for LMCA and Roto-Rooter was to license the Roto-Rooter name for a new drain cleaner. As we creatively explored the market potential for this drain cleaner in the ideation session, we realized it could be much more than a licensed property: it could be a unique business-building idea for all Roto-Rooter franchisees across the United States. The idea was to offer a money-back guarantee for the Roto-Rooter drain cleaner, and thus provide a potential competitive advantage over Liquid Plumr or Drano. What made the idea particularly clever was not the money-back guarantee but that if the drain cleaner didn't work, consumers could get the entire cost of the drain cleaner refunded immediately by the local Roto-Rooter man, who would be more than happy to do so. He could then, presumably, be hired by that same consumer to professionally clear the still-clogged drain.

#8 Company Acquisitions Thought Experiments

If your company had the wherewithal and the desire to acquire any other company on the planet, which would it choose? Would it be within your industry or outside it? Or if that's too fantastical a notion, then consider if your company were going to be acquired by another one. What company would you want to be the acquirer? Whether you're the acquirer or acquiree, these acquisition thought experiments can be a rich source of new product ideas, new business strategies, and new distribution models.

Let's say you're the Vermont-based coffee company Green Mountain. Their acquisition of the coffee-maker company Keurig has given it a huge competitive advantage over other coffee companies by providing an additional outlet for selling its coffee in Keurig's convenient single-serve K-cups. But what's next? What would happen if Green Mountain were bought by (or more fantastically, bought) Sony? or Amazon? or McDonald's? or even Starbucks? How would its business model change? What new products could you imagine it offering if it were either acquired by or acquired WeightWatchers? If you ever find yourself or your team in a less-than-productive phase, essentially trying to till the same ground that's already been worked over for many years, this technique is guaranteed to get you out of your mental rut and quickly launch you into previously unimagined new fields of opportunity.

#9 Product Acquisitions

One of the more interesting new product ideation sessions I've ever facilitated was for a company that specializes in over-the-counter (OTC) medicines. Since many of its product categories were regulated by the Food and Drug Administration (FDA), which dictates which active ingredients a company can use and what performance claims it can make for them (assuming it doesn't want to go through the multi-million-dollar expense of filing a new drug application), it's a tremendous creative challenge to find meaningful competitive points of difference. One strategy is to stay within the FDA requirements yet potentially provide added consumer benefits by offering products in different forms or more convenient dispensing systems. Think of the change that has taken place in sun care products. They used to be just "gunk in a bottle." Now they are available in foams, sticks, and gels, and dispensed through aerosol sprays or pumps, making it much more pleasant and convenient to use them and therefore more likely that adults and children will.

This manufacturer of OTC products was looking for secondary brands that it could acquire. These were brands that had at least some brand awareness and brand equity with consumers, but may have been on the decline for years due to lessening product quality, lack of advertising or promotion, more competition or innovation in the category, or a host of other reasons. Our new product strategy was to ideate creative ways to combine these old brands with new technologies that the company already owned: new product forms or new dispensing systems. The session identified more than a dozen brands for possible acquisition and ultimately the company bought a sun care brand.

#10 R&D Cross-Pollination

If your company is large enough, joint ideation sessions between different R&D functions and departments can help you and your team get an entirely new perspective on your product category, as well as lead you down new and interesting research directions.

You should also not reject out of hand the idea of cross-company R&D ideation sessions. While it may not be easy to write the intellectual property agreement (it took months to agree on the contract in a joint ideation session I facilitated for Unilever and Black and Decker), the ideation opportunities for both companies can be tremendously exciting. For a company specializing in personal care liquids and creams, to be able to think about adding devices to their product offerings holds great potential. And for a device company to be able to possibly leverage the formulation know-how and brand strength of a personal care company is equally exciting.

Of course, it's also possible to do a joint R&D ideation session exercise without even having the other company there. Freelance R&D experts can take the place of the other company's experts. And for any joint innovation project that is conceived using these outside experts, contract manufacturers can also be hired to produce the new "joint company" product.

#11 Global Product Scans and Trend Identification

Let's say you are in the business of inventing new food products. How can you discover trends that could help you? A number of research houses specialize in creating a database of recently introduced products from around the world. Mintel is probably the best known, and best, of these research houses. Its online database of new food products includes not only pictures of the product, but ingredient and nutrition labels as well, and it is now possible to search the company's database by key words. Key word searches (semantic trend analysis, as we call it) make it fairly easy to know which ingredients and nutritional claims are hot around the world and which are not. Is using sea salt as an ingredient an emerging trend? If so, where? How about pomegranate juice? Pure cane sugar versus artificial sweeteners? What about individually wrapped packages for added convenience or portion control? Which categories of products are focusing on natural ingredients? What's happening with organic foods? This knowledge can be leveraged to inspire new product ideas, as well as product formulations.

In addition to semantic trend analysis, we recommend using three other trend approaches to identify exciting food trends and possible innovations that could be inspired by them: Internet restaurant menu scans, recipe scans (using field trips to restaurants), and nutritionist and "foodie" interviews (including inviting chefs, nutritional experts, and food magazine writers to ideation sessions).

#12 Customer and Trade Outreach

As retailers become more and more sophisticated about how they profile and segment their shoppers (through sales data, social media, and loyalty programs), they can help manufacturers know where to fish for new ideas by letting them know which categories may be hot or ripe for innovation. Occasionally they suggest some great new product ideas—other times, some not so great ideas. One large retailer, for instance, suggested to the Suave brand team that consumers might like a lower-cost but still high-quality toothpaste. It was not a good idea, as consumer research later validated. But retailers can often make a good idea even better. I'm thinking of a new product introduction we worked on for Thomas' Mini Squares Bagelbread. Originally we had thought it made sense to market the product in a plastic clamshell package. Walmart encouraged us to put it in a more Earth-friendly cardboard tray, and as it turned out, they were right. Not only was the package idea better for the environment, it helped convey an image of authentic home-baked goodness that Thomas' is famous for.

Having conducted joint ideation sessions between manufacturers and such retailers as Sam's Club, Target, CVS, and Home Depot, I can say with confidence that the smartest manufacturers see retailers as integral partners in their new product efforts. A case in point is a new product display program that our innovation agency client Bimbo Bakeries has pioneered in Walmart Supercenters. Knowing that the bread aisle is a relatively low-involvement aisle with a high degree of automatic, grab-and-go shopping behavior, Bimbo and Walmart have created a permanently fixtured, dedicated new product display entitled

"What's HOT in baking?" On the display is a wide assortment of the new products that we are continually helping Bimbo to create.

#13 Trade Shows and Events

Walking the floor of your industry's trade shows can be a source of great ideas. A less obvious but equally important idea-finding strategy is to go to trade shows outside your industry as well. These shows can be a great source of new structural packaging ideas, product claims and language, joint venture or copromotion or comarketing ideas, and new research approaches and methodologies. For new food ideas, we might go to a vitamin and supplements trade show, a cosmetics and toiletries trade show, an inventor's trade show, or even a home and garden trade show.

Beyond the packaging, new product claims, and comarketing ideas that you might get from walking the trade show exhibit halls, trade shows can also be a unique opportunity to elicit ideas from industry experts, your own (sales) people, or even brokers. This was the case with one of our clients that markets high-quality cheese. During an industry trade show, where over forty of the company's national network of food brokers were in attendance, we designed and facilitated a three-hour ideation session. It was an inexpensive way for our client to generate a wide variety of new marketing, product, and merchandising ideas. For instance, an idea to copromote cheese in the produce and fresh fruit sections of a large supermarket chain, creating crudités and cheese or fruit and cheese plates for entertaining, came out of this session.

#14 Category Analogues and Cross-Category Products

Think of the creative mind-set principle-finding, principle-transfer from Chapter One, and you'll have the essence of this creative approach. Category analogues is simply a matter of looking to categories other than your own for concepts, principles, ingredients, packaging, forms, and formulas that you can transfer back to your category to inspire new ideas.

A good example of this creative strategy in action was a new product ideation session I facilitated for a famous cookie company that resulted in one of the highest-scoring, best-tasting, most exciting new product lines I have ever seen. The goal of the ideation session was to generate high-quality, indulgent, new cookie ideas. To help trigger the group's thinking in the brainwalk exercise, I used dozens of pictures of interesting dessert concoctions culled from a variety of dessert cookbooks. In this very successful exercise, one idea in particular stood out. A visual of a scrumptious ice cream dessert concoction got the group thinking of ice cream and ice cream flavors as inspiration for a new line of cookies. Would there be a way to create a line of cookies that took their names, flavors, colors, and creamy texture from some of the most popular flavors of ice cream?

As the group explored this possibility of a line of cookies inspired by ice cream flavors and exactly how they could be designed and manufactured, the excitement for the idea grew. The group settled on a beautifully crafted cookie "wheel" filled with the "ice cream": a wonderful Oreo-like (ice)-"cream filling." Ultimately the new cookie line was offered in a variety of decadent ice cream flavors: cookies and crème, mint chocolate, chocolate almond, and pralines and crème. I still think that these were some of the best cookies I have ever tasted.

And maybe it was because they did taste so good that the line ultimately didn't succeed. The highest-quality ingredients meant a high cost of goods, which translated to a high retail selling price. They were launched in a recessionary time and never found their market. But it was still a great idea, as evidenced by record concept test scores. The strength of the tested concept demonstrated that if you can find the right analogue, it may lead you to a great idea, assuming you can get the price right.

So if you're trying to invent a new cookie, think about ice cream. If you're inventing a new ice cream, consider candy. If you're looking for new candy ideas, think gum. And if you're trying to invent a new gum, why not consider cookies?

#15 New Business Models and Channels

How about a chain of Entenmann's bake shops along America's highways? Or a water delivery company that also conducts home-use-testing research? Or a detergent company that creates customized scented detergents that are ordered online and delivered? These are the kinds of ideas and opportunity platforms that can come from thinking of your product or service through the lens of a new business model, including direct marketing or online, home delivery, a store within a store, or institutional- or manufacturer-owned retail product stores.

Many years ago, before newspapers fell on hard times because of the loss of classified advertising revenues, we were hired to do creative future scenario planning work for a famous Midwestern newspaper. As we explored the ramifications of how new technologies and the Internet could change the world of newspaper advertising, and then got creative about how to exploit these inevitable changes, it became clear that the newspaper had two fundamental growth (some might say survival) strategies. It could invent new ways to monetize its core competency of generating original, timely, and valuable information, or it could leverage its current infrastructure and competency for efficiently delivering "things" to people's homes and businesses.

If your company is struggling because technology is making your product or service obsolete, it's probably not a bad idea to start thinking creatively about new business models.

#16 Brand Extensions and Equity Migrations

These days, most companies have a vision. An interesting creative exercise is also to create a vision for each of the company's brands. In the brand vision work we have done for packaged goods brands, we have found that the most effective techniques are those that encourage the session participants to anthropomorphize the brand: they pretend that the brand is a person and then allow the brand to "speak for itself." What would the brand say its unique reason for being in this world is? If the brand were going to give a speech, what would it say? If the brand were going to share with you its fondest dream, what would that dream be? If the brand were going to tell you how it's going to improve the world, what would it say?

This work to get at the brand vision, as well as the brand's personality, has the added advantage of helping to identify the brand's equity and how far this equity could be extended in offering new products or services. If All detergent sees itself as the friendly and fun family cleaner or helper, could All also be a line of household cleaners? Could All be a line of family-friendly, easy-to-use cleaning tools? How about an All car wax? Or an All house cleaning service? As the brand vision team uses these imagined products and services to identify what's in and, as important, what's out, a much clearer picture of the current brand's equity, as well as how far that equity could be creatively extended into other new products and businesses, begins to emerge.

The Attitudes of Successful Innovation

So those are our sweet sixteen thinking strategies, methodologies, or approaches. We have found that all sixteen can be rich sources of new product ideas and innovative business growth strategies. If you choose to incorporate them in your innovation program, you should know that we believe there are three attitudinal prerequisites to using them successfully.

First, to do innovation well requires a great deal of hard work. (Working the sixteen idea-finding, thought-starting categories is only the first step in the three-step process I'm recommending for facilitating leaders: step 2 is creating opportunity area platforms, and step 3 is iterative insight mining.) It is critical that senior management understand that the company's innovation program is not a once- or twice-a-year event where everyone gets together for a full and fun day of ideation to fill this year's new product development pipeline. A successful innovation program requires constant effort and vigilance: an ongoing, day-in and day-out commitment by a dedicated team of employees and supportive suppliers doing the hard work of idea creation and development.

Second, it's important to know and accept that the work of innovation, unlike a well-developed manufacturing or production process, is inefficient. Most of your innovation work will lead nowhere. There must be continuous experimentation and learning, recognizing that even with the false starts, wrong paths, and dead-ends, valuable things are being learned and important experience is being gained that ultimately will serve the innovation team well. Successful and repeatable innovation requires making many smaller bets, most of which won't pay out, before you can identify which ideas in your portfolio of ideas could be the big in-market winners. Consequently, your innovation program must operate in an environment where there is both a philosophical acceptance of the inherent inefficiency of any innovation process and adequate staffing and funding for the process to bear fruit.

Finally, you should think of these sixteen innovation approaches and thinking categories only as creative starting points. They are not a formula for innovation success because no such formula exists. They are best-in-class process suggestions that help creative and impassioned innovators know where and how to fish for new, occasionally breakthrough ideas. But at the end of the day, it'll be in your practice of the art of innovation and your and your team's unique collection of cross-functional talents that will help you succeed at the hard work of innovation. In other words, you will need to be creative about how you explore and leverage the sixteen categories of innovation thinking for your company and industry. Indeed, you may discover that several (or even many) of these innovation approaches are not right for your company. Conversely, you may also discover that by combining some of these innovation thinking approaches, as we often do on behalf of our clients, will inspire even more innovation thinking and innovation growth opportunities for you and your company.

creating opportunity areas platforms

The sixteen approaches will send you on fishing trips that will enable you and your innovation team to identify a wide array of insights, opportunity areas, ideation stimuli, preliminary ideas, and growth strategies. All of these inputs can then be used to help inspire and focus ongoing ideation sessions. These sessions should enable the innovation team not only to generate a wide variety of new ideas but also to identify category themes, patterns, and trends.

These themes, patterns, and trends form the basis of what we call opportunity area platforms. These platforms, as the name implies, are groups of ideas, insights, or even wishes that could be the basis for new categories of new products. Qualitative research will then be used to determine which opportunity area platforms might have the greatest potential for meeting important unmet consumer needs.

Let's say that you are in the nonalcoholic beverage business. Your preliminary fishing trips have helped you uncover stimuli, new ideas, and trends that have led you to create the following sixteen opportunity-area platforms:

1. Health beverages
2. Energy beverages
3. Exotic ingredient beverages
4. Beverages that have a dessert analogue (for example, ice cream sodas)
5. Beverages with a vitamin analogue or ingredient
6. Breakfast beverages
7. Lunch, snack, or dinner beverages
8. After-dinner or nighttime beverages
9. Sports beverages
10. Coffee or tea beverages
11. Fruit beverages
12. Licensable property beverages (perhaps a child's drink named after a cartoon character)
13. Water variants (distilled, fortified, added flavors, and so on)
14. Weight-loss beverages
15. New beverage packaging or delivery vehicles
16. Beverages for women

This is not meant to be an exhaustive list of possible platforms. For one client, for instance, we generated 110 opportunity area platforms in our initial round of work. Nor are these platforms meant to be mutually exclusive. Health drinks, for instance, may be too broad a category to be creatively or strategically useful. Yogurt is perceived as healthy. Could you make and market a line of refreshing yogurt shakes, targeted to on-the-go teens to replace soda or iced tea? Should these yogurt shakes fall under a broader "health drinks" platform, or should it be its own platform?

The who, what, where, how, and why formula that helped categorize the sixteen thinking approaches can also be used to help generate other platforms that the original idea fishing trips did not. For instance:

- Who else might be interested in specialized beverages? People with diabetes? Hispanics? Newborns? Menopausal women? Baby boomers with sore joints?
- When specifically might someone want a specialized beverage? Before a test? After a meal as a digestion aid? How about as a weight-loss aid?
- Where might someone want or need a new kind of beverage? While commuting? In the office? At the gym? On a ski slope? Where might the beverage have been sourced or made: the Amazon jungle? the desert? a glacier?
- What is it uniquely made of? What might uniquely be added to a beverage? Heat? Suspended flavor crystals?
- What kinds of packages could make drinking beverages more fun? Exciting? Convenient?
- How might the beverage be specially produced? In space? Under pressure? In a microwave? On a griddle? Inside a tree?

Next, the innovation team will want to start prioritizing these platforms based on a variety of strategic considerations and questions:

- Will anyone want this product or care about it?
- Could this be an exciting new platform for us?

- Do we have a brand it could be marketed under, or do we have to create a new brand?
- Is it unique?
- Will it have broad appeal, or is it too much of a niche product?
- Is it a single product, or could it be a line of products?
- Can we distribute it using our current distribution system, or will we need to use or create a new channel of distribution?
- What kind of margins can we get?

The innovation team can then start ideating specific new product ideas for each of the highest-potential platforms. The ideas that are generated within each of these platforms can be taken to consumers for further learning and validation.

iterative insight mining

You've gone fishing for new ideas using the sixteen thinking strategies and grouped these ideas into opportunity area platforms. You've ideated new product ideas within the most promising of these platforms. You may have even preliminarily focus-group-tested, with target market consumers, several of the new product ideas that came out of your focused ideation sessions. As the new product innovation team, are you done?

Actually you're only just getting started. Now the real work, and the true art, of new product development begins. You and your team have to work diligently to make sure you get all the elements of the new product mix right: the name, product positioning, pricing, claims, package, product quality, how it's sold to the trade and merchandised for the consumer, and how its unique (and, you hope, motivating) consumer benefit is communicated through advertising, promotion, and public relations to consumers. Get even one of these elements of the product mix wrong, and most likely you will have a failure. The complexity of getting all these elements right, especially for a truly breakthrough product, where most everything is new, can be daunting since there are so many critical creative decisions at each stage of the new product development process. It's not hard to see why eight or nine out of every ten new consumer products fail.

More than three out of five of the new products we work on succeed; this is because we do what we call iterative insight mining. At its heart, the theory behind our process is simple and can be summarized in seven words: keep working until you get it right. Specifically, this means that it's important to go back and forth between ideation, consumer input and testing, and product improvements until all the elements of the new product mix come together in an integrated and compelling proposition for the consumer.

Time and performance pressures, combined with the difficult creative challenge of getting all the elements of the new product mix right, make it tempting to start compromising critical components of the idea. Of course, in the creation of any new product, successful or not, there will be compromises and trade-offs. It's the nature of the beast, particularly when you are trying to balance performance with considerations of price value. The trick is knowing which trade-offs you can give on and which you can't. And it should be the consumer, not R&D or sales or manufacturing, who has the final say-so on these "allowable" trade-offs.

At each phase of the new product development process, we refine and, if need be, reinvent the elements of the mix until we feel, and consumers tell us, that we have a winning new product concept. This iterative process takes time and money and a lot of hard work. And it requires the team to be creative problem solvers throughout the entire new product development process. But that's what makes it fun and rewarding, especially when you get it right— which you will, more times than not, if you keep checking in with the consumer.

A good example of getting it right was a new product initiative that my partner, Gary Fraser, led in the toothbrush category. Following the success of his team's creation of Mentadent toothpaste, Gary charged the team with inventing a better toothbrush. Since the Mentadent brand was already becoming known for doing innovative things in the oral care category, a "me-too," minor-improvement toothbrush was not going to do it. The team's goal was to create something great, with an important consumer point of difference and benefit.

The team began the process. They talked to consumers about their brushing habits. They watched consumers brush their teeth through two-way mirrors. They conducted their own internal ideation sessions to begin generating new product ideas.

As the team worked, they discovered an important insight about the way people brush: people brush all wrong. For one, they don't brush far enough back in the mouth, so many of the molars were not being brushed properly, if at all. Another problem was that people were often brushing their teeth horizontally, or side to side, when they should be brushing their teeth up and down. One of the advantages of brushing the teeth vertically is that the brush head is more likely to clean under and around the gums and thus promote gum health. Since Mentadent was becoming known for its care of not only teeth but gums as well, this seemed like a rich opportunity area: inventing a toothbrush that promoted better gum health.

Further consumer research validated that not only would consumers want to buy a specially designed toothbrush that promoted gum health, but that they'd be willing to pay a premium for it. The challenge was that to truly promote better brushing and gum health, people would have to change their current brushing behavior. Would they? Knowing how difficult it can be to change behavior, the team set the inventive goal for itself of creating a toothbrush that would do a better job of cleaning teeth and gums without having to change current brushing behavior.

Now that the creative challenge was defined, the team could focus the iterative new product development process—going back and forth between consumer research and design ideation—much more efficiently and effectively. They also added an important outside partner in the development process: a design firm that had industrial designers who specialized in designing precision instruments for surgeons.

The industrial designers created dozens of prototypes for consumers to try. They were also encouraged to become an integral part of the consumer research process. Not only were they watching consumers brush and react to their designs, they were asked to conduct interviews as well. By interacting with consumers directly, they could understand what was and wasn't working with their designs.

The team came up with four major improvements to the toothbrush as it then existed, most of which have now become standard in the category. To help the brusher get the bristles to clean around and underneath the gums, the designers angled or fanned the bristles. This allowed the bristles, when they came in contact with the tooth in the course of side-to-side brushing, to naturally bow or flex downward and clean the gums. The designers also created a special set of angled brushes at the very end of the toothbrush that made it easy (in fact, impossible not to) clean the molar teeth at the back of the mouth. Third, the team created a special handle with indentations for the fingers, as well as rubberized material within these indentations, to make it easier to grip the toothbrush and prevent it from moving in the hand, so that the angled bristles would brush where they were meant to. The fourth improvement was purely aesthetic: they made the handle out of a high-tech, see-through plastic to help send the message that this was indeed something revolutionary in the world of toothbrushes.

The results were spectacular. The Mentadent toothbrush became an instant $50 million-a-year success. It was also put on display, where it resides to this day, at the Cooper-Hewitt Museum in New York City as an example of award-winning design.

■ ■ ■

So these are the three processes—idea fishing, platform development, and iterative insight mining—that I recommend using to improve the quantity, quality, and, most important, the success rates of your new product and new business creation and development programs. In the next chapter, we'll look at some of the practical and proven ideation techniques and innovation processes that can help you and your team generate winning ideas for specific elements of the new product marketing mix, as well as ideation techniques I've developed to address business challenges outside of new products.

5

real-world challenges
applying ideation techniques and innovation processes

The preceding chapters have explored a range of mind-sets, thinking strategies, creative techniques, and idea development methodologies, all of which can be used to address a wide variety of innovation challenges. As we get into the practical application of different ideation and innovation techniques, the question arises whether some techniques are better than others for addressing specific kinds of business challenges. The simple answer is yes.

The first half of this chapter shows how to match and customize specific techniques to generate ideas for specific kinds of business challenges. I have included four expected classes of creative business challenges: creating product positionings, generating promotion and advertising ideas, inventing new products, and creating new product names. The second half of the chapter consists of accounts of several business challenges my company and I were presented with that either are not typically addressed with individual or group ideation techniques or that led to the creation of new, powerful tools for ideation and innovation. These stories—about a culture change initiative, a sales forecasting challenge, a new tool for growth strategizing, and a new tool for group ideating without a group session—give insight into the ways that creative ideation techniques and approaches can potentially catalyze solutions for virtually any imaginable business challenge.

Let's start by seeing which ideation techniques and innovation processes I've discovered, through a great deal of trial and error, work best for positioning, promotion, product development, and naming. (In this chapter, I do not specifically address all of the ideation techniques noted, but I do elsewhere in the book.)

challenge: product positioning

Key Techniques: Worst Idea; Picture Prompts, Target-Market/ Role Play with Triggered Brainwalk; Headliner and Headliner Alternative

When I am facilitating a creative positioning ideation session, I sometimes begin the session by asking, "By the way, what is a positioning anyway?" Then I'll prompt the group further by asking some follow-on questions: "Is a positioning a tagline?" "Is it a product claim of superior performance?" "Is the essence of a positioning a better reason to believe?" "Could a positioning be reflected in a great brand name like 'Lean Cuisine'?"

All of these could certainly be elements of a positioning. But to my mind, a positioning is much simpler than that. A positioning is the one thing above all else you'd like consumers to think about your brand. And that one thing should be unique and compelling in some important way to your target market consumers. It's not easy to create a winning positioning, especially in an increasingly competitive and overcommunicated world.

One of the misconceptions about positioning work is that you can analyze your way to a winning positioning. The notion that by first gathering all relevant facts and data and then, by thinking through the available information logically, a unique, ownable, and compelling positioning will emerge, is simply not true. The art of positioning can't be reduced to a science of positioning. You're still going to need that missing element known as creativity.

This is not to say that the research and analytics are not important in laying the foundation for creating a great positioning. They are. Indeed they are critical. Being intimately familiar with the following are all-important in creating a unique and compelling brand positioning:

- The equities or heritage of your own brand (assuming that it's not a new brand)
- The equities and positionings of competitive brands
- The product category consumer needs, drivers, and consumer motivators and benefits
- Which market segment within the broader universe of consumers the brand is trying to reach or appeal to the most

But they are only that: first steps. With these facts and findings on hand (and in head), it's time to get creative. And the best creative ideation techniques for positioning are picture prompts, worst idea, target market/role play combined with triggered brainwalk, and the best of the best, Headliner (or its alternative).

Worst Idea

For a one-day positioning ideation session I designed and facilitated for Old El Paso salsa, we used a half-dozen creative techniques to stimulate new thinking and ideas. Interestingly, it was the worst idea technique that was most inspiring to one of the agency creatives in the session, whose bad idea was, "Why don't we have a fat guy dance around singing 'Nacho Nacho Man' instead of 'Macho Macho Man'?"

It's wonderful having ad agency creatives in an ideation session because they'll often say something so far out in left field—typically as a wisecrack or joke—that it can't help but open up the session to new creative possibilities. In this case, it was the worst idea technique that helped liberate this very funny, off-the-wall, half-joking idea. However, precisely because the idea was so funny, I suspect that had it emerged at any time during the day other than during the worst idea technique, we might have missed its important positioning implications. It would have just been a good laugh that helped us loosen up and was then forgotten. But by working to turn this worst idea into a good idea, it became clear that implicit in the irreverent "Nacho Nacho Man" concept was an exciting positioning possibility: to position Old El Paso salsa as the ultimate nacho-making ingredient. A significant percentage of salsa in the U.S. market is indeed used for making nachos, so why not own this use for Old El Paso salsa?

And although it should never be the primary consideration for picking one positioning over another, it was certainly a bonus that the hard work of creating an idea to communicate this positioning within a memorable and compelling thirty-second commercial was already done. At the end of the day, literally and figuratively, the nacho positioning proved to be the most macho of all the ideas the group created. And if you ever saw the commercial, I think you'd agree that it isn't one you'd soon forget.

Headliner and Headliner Alternative

Of course, the worst idea is only one of several important creative positioning techniques. In my experience, the most powerful of all the positioning ideation techniques is one we call the headliner technique (now the headliner alternative technique). Headliner is a computer program that contains over ninety thousand phrases, taglines, book titles, headlines, and slogans. The database is searchable by key words, so that the facilitating leader can preselect, and use as thought prompts, expressions that are directly related to a brand's current or hoped-for equity. As such, Headliner is a great example of a focused ideation technique. It promotes blue sky thinking while simultaneously firmly grounding the creative thinking in a brand or category's key benefits or essences.

Unfortunately, the Headliner program is no longer for sale. However, the good news is that because of the power of the Internet, there is an equally powerful, and free, alternative. You can get virtually the same results of a key word Headliner search (generating expressions, book titles, clichés, and so on) by searching key words using the following online databases:

- General interest quote search: http://www.brainyquote.com/ and http://www.quotemountain.com/
- Literature and poetry databases: http://www.bartleby.com /quotations/
- Movie quotes: http://www.subzin.com/ and http://www.imdb.com /search/text
- Clichés: http://www.clichefinder.com/ and http://www.westegg .com/cliche/
- Advertising taglines and more general quotes: http://en.wikiquote .org and www.thinkexist.com

To see how to use expressions, movie titles, clichés, and so on that contain your key words to inspire new positioning ideas, let's look at an example of a positioning session I facilitated for a famous headache remedy.

For my computer search of the Headliner database, I used key words associated with both the brand and the headache category: *strong, pain, fast,* and *relief.* Expressions that emerged from the search included "Stronger Than Red Devil Lye," "Growing Pains," "Think Fast, Mr. Moto," and "Relief with the Touch of Your Hand." These expressions, hundreds of them, were then passed out to the session participants to help inspire new positioning ideas for the headache remedy. Notice that I said "inspire an idea," not "provide an idea." The expressions themselves rarely provide an answer. Rather, they should be viewed as creative thought starters to help a team create new and interesting positioning ideas (or taglines) for a particular product.

Facilitating this technique is an easy four-step process:

1. Pass out a page or two of expressions to each participant. Everyone in the room will have different expressions.

2. Have individuals, working alone, circle several expressions that they find interesting.
3. Form small teams that share their circled expressions with each other.
4. Use these circled expressions to encourage everyone on the team to generate and share new positioning ideas.

For example, seeing the expression, "Think Fast, Mr. Moto," might inspire one team member to propose a positioning that linked headache relief with the ability to make quicker and better decisions. "Think Fast, Mr. Moto" might inspire another team member to suggest positioning the product specifically for working men (Mr. Moto) who can't afford downtime at work because of a headache.

Another example of the headliner technique in action was a positioning session I facilitated for Oral-B electric toothbrushes. The key words I used in searching the database were *clean, dentist, mouth, oral, brush,* and *smile.* Some of the expressions and thought prompts that came out of this search included these:

- Cleans as It Lubricates
- Beauty by the Brushful
- A Brush with Greatness
- Afraid of Dentists? Try Us, We're Gentle
- Miles of Smiles
- For a Clean That Shines
- Brush Up
- Don't Look a Gift Horse in the Mouth
- Discover America. It's 3,000 Smiles Wide.
- The Way Some Dentists Make You Wait, No Wonder You're Called the Patient

The ideation session participants then used these expressions to trigger new positioning ideas and taglines. Of the more than seven hundred ideas that came out of that day's session (a record), many of the best ideas came from this exercise, including the winning idea (in the form of a tagline): "Brush like a Dentist." Among the different expressions of this same idea were:

- B-Smart, Brush like a Dentist
- Brush like a Dentist, Smile Like the King/Queen
- Trust Your Brush, and Brush Like a Dentist
- Healthier Mouth, Healthier Life: Brush Like a Dentist.

As it turned out, Oral-B's advertising agency at the time, BBDO, had come up with the same "Brush like a Dentist" tagline on their own and would soon convince the Oral-B management team that this was the way to go.

This technique works so well in positioning ideation for several reasons:

- Because the technique is so stimuli rich, with scores of relevant key word expressions for each participant, it is easy to immediately start generating new connections and ideas.
- Since it uses brand- and category-relevant stimuli and key words, the ideas that are generated tend to be more focused and strategically aligned.
- The stimuli are in a form: expressions, idioms, and taglines, which are closely related to the desired output—taglines that reflect a new positioning. As such, at least in creative terms, it's often easier for like to inspire like.

challenge: advertising and promotion

Key Techniques: Wishing, Promotion Prompts, Headliner Alternatives, and Category Analogues

I've grouped creating advertising and promotion ideas together as similar creative challenges because these two methods and mediums for getting your product and brand noticed have a lot in common if they are done well. Great ads communicate a product benefit and brand essence in a unique, memorable, and motivating way. Great promotions do, too. Happily, the ideation techniques for creating great ads works equally well for creating great promotions.

The creative mind-sets in Chapter One, which should serve you well in creating breakthrough advertising and promotion ideas, are creator of worlds and principle-finding/principle transfer. And the ideation techniques most closely associated with each of these mind-sets are wishing for creator of worlds and promotion prompts and category analogues for principle finding/principle transfer.

Wishing

A good example of wishing in the world of promotion was an ideation and innovation training session my partner and I ran for luxury goods manufacturer Louis Vuitton Moet Hennessey. To launch a new, high-end perfume with a limited promotion budget, we encouraged session participants to forget about the small budget and "wish for the impossible." The prompt led to the fantastical idea of having it "rain perfume" by either misting the fragrance off buildings in New York City or spraying it from airplanes.

Promotion Prompts

For the facilitating leader, promotion prompts is an easy technique to facilitate and is particularly useful when a team needs extra help to generate creative and different, but also practical and doable, promotional ideas. Every year for over twenty years, *Promo* magazine has given awards for the best promotions of the year. Known as the PRO awards, there are first-, second-, and third-place awards, as well as honorable mentions, in twenty-three promotion categories, including Best Use of Event Marketing; Best Cause-Based Promotion; Best Web-Based Promotion; Best Mobile Marketing Campaign; Best Use of Games, Contests and Sweepstakes; Best Sampling Program; Best Campaign on a Budget (Under $250,000); and even Best Campaign That Uses a Holiday Theme in Its Promotion. These award-winning promotion ideas, with short write-ups of specifically how they worked, are available on line, free of charge, at *Promo* magazine's Web site.

For more than a dozen years, I have used these award-winning promotions as triggers for helping my clients generate new promotional ideas. In the ideation session, I pass out copies of these promotions (typically I give three to four different ones to each session participant) and ask them, alone or in small teams, to figure out how they might adapt or modify one of the ideas in the handouts to help them create a new promotional idea for their particular brand. It's not only simple but effective.

Category Analogues

Transferring ideas from one category to another can lead to breakthrough concepts, including the world of advertising and promotion. A good example using category analogues successfully was a joint advertising and promotion ideation session for Ford.

The car was the Ford Focus. Fusion 5, a creative advertising and marketing company in Westport, Connecticut, asked me to help it design and facilitate a series of ideation sessions with its own company creatives and outside experts. Fusion 5's cofounder, Patrick Meyer, and president, Dave Moran, had what I thought was a brilliant strategy for generating the breakthrough creative advertising and promotion ideas we were all hoping for from the session. Why not think of the launch of a car metaphorically, much as you might think of a launch of, say, a new movie? Or the launch of the fall collection from a major fashion designer? And so for each of the three sessions I facilitated, we focused on a different launch analogue (film, fragrance, fashion) and invited different experts to each. For example, for the movie launch session, Fusion 5 recruited executives from several of the major movie studios to help us brainstorm.

Since the car was targeted to younger buyers, Fusion 5 also invited some hip New York City young adults: fun, creative, antiauthoritarian, urban cool people. Interestingly, the differences in the group—older executives, young adults, Fusion 5 creatives and account people—worked to our creative advantage. It created both a healthy tension and a kind of creative oneupmanship. Paradoxically, when the group began to share in the excitement of creating truly breakthrough ideas together, it also brought the group together in a magical sort of way.

These sessions were three of the best I have ever facilitated. Ultimately the ideas generated in the three sessions helped make the launch of the Ford Focus one of the most successful ever in the history of the car business. We'll look at just two of the implemented ideas that came out of the brainstorm session with the movie executives.

The Ford Focus is beautifully designed and engineered: it's a small, affordable economy car but with lots of space inside for passengers. As we explored the richness of the movie-launch metaphor, we began to imagine a Hollywood premiere of a major motion picture: red carpets, spotlights at night, lines of people waiting to get in, VIPs only. Since we quickly realized that the car was our main attraction, the big idea was to have people not waiting to see what was in the theater but rather the car itself. It was this insight that led to the highly successful TV commercial. The ad was a direct translation of the movie premiere idea, red carpet and all, with people cordoned off waiting to see which celebrities would get out of the car. And since the car had so much room inside, a large collection of very attractive, heavily blinged young women stepped out of the car, ultimately followed by one heavily blinged guy, who was also just plain heavy.

The second idea, a promotional and PR idea that anticipated the trend in both reality TV and do-it-yourself, YouTube types of videos, also was inspired by the movie metaphor. The idea was to equip young adults with video cameras and send them on a cross-country driving tour of the United States documenting their adventures in their new Ford Focus. The tour provided great footage for PR and promotional purposes that both reinforced the target market for the car (younger adults) and the comfort and extra room to move inside it.

Of course, as in any other ideation session, only a small number of the ideas created were implemented. One of my favorite (which still has not seen the light of day) was suggested by one of the younger urban cool participants. He wanted Ford to hold a contest in all five New York City boroughs to find the team of teenagers who could strip the Focus in the fastest time. What better way to demonstrate the car's unique features and the extra room inside than to take the car completely apart? (Remember the saying that if an idea doesn't make you at least a little nervous, it probably isn't a big idea.)

The Ford Focus project is a good example of how powerful category analogues can be in generating ideas in the world of promotion and advertising. Another example of using category analogues to solve creative business challenges can be found in the naming section of this chapter. But before we get to that, we first need to learn strategies and techniques for generating the new product ideas themselves.

challenge: new products and extending the brand

Key Techniques: Many

We use approximately two dozen new product ideation techniques in our new product ideation sessions. These techniques include triggered brainwalking, worst idea, patent prompts, questioning assumptions, twenty questions, picture prompts, magazine rip and rap, semantic intuition, target market wishing, YouTube videos, day in the life, and customized movie clips, along with the concept development technique of billboarding (see Chapter Six). Chapter Nine details several of these techniques in action and how to select, choreograph, and facilitate them in a new product ideation session extending over a day and a half.

With all these new product ideation techniques to choose from, it might surprise you that some of the more successful new product ideas we've worked on didn't come from new product ideation sessions at all. Rather, they came from other kinds of ideation sessions, such as a positioning session, a brand vision session, a product claims session, a trade marketing session, or even a strategy session where lucky accidents led to a new product idea. How and why did these lucky accidents happen?

With the cost of developing a new brand so high, most consumer product companies are working hard to exploit and leverage the awareness and equity of their established master brands. Certainly introducing new flavors, ingredients, package sizes, or delivery systems under an existing brand makes a great deal of sense. But companies are also introducing very different innovations, or even new product breakthroughs, under these master brands. Oreo Cakesters, Arnold's Sandwich Thins, Trident Layers gum, Apple's "i" naming strategy (for pads, pods, and phones), and even Procter & Gamble's chain of Mr. Clean Car Washes are good examples of leveraging a master brand instead of investing heavily to create a new one.

Consequently we are increasingly being asked to design and facilitate sessions to understand and leverage a brand's current and potential equity. Creating a new positioning to reinvigorate the sales of a sleepy but well-regarded brand, generating new claims to give that brand a new competitive advantage, or working on a creative new merchandising program to increase the brand's presence at the shelf are all effective strategies for helping the marketing and sales teams realize a brand's potential. By encouraging brand teams to think more creatively about their brands in all of these areas and more, new product ideas often emerge. It's a phenomenon reminiscent of the old expression, "The harder I work [on my brand], the luckier I get!"

challenge: naming

Key Techniques: Random Stimuli; Collaging; Picture Prompts; Category Alternatives; Tagline Triggers

An innovation consulting colleague once said to me that he thought naming was easy. And it is, but only if you're willing to settle for a lousy name. Creating a great name, even a good name, is tough. Indeed, I think it is one of the most difficult of all the classes of creative business challenges. It's especially hard in these times of product and service name proliferation because when you finally do get that flash of creative naming brilliance and come up with what seems to be the perfect name, you discover that some other company or individual has registered it, and so it's not available. But what choice is there? Unless you decide you're going to adopt Prince's "product formerly known as . . ." anti-naming strategy, there aren't any alternatives. Your product or service needs a name.

Naming is one of the few areas where we use random techniques and stimuli in addition to more focused ideation techniques. We try whatever technique or mental strategy we can to create a name we like, and there's no way to know which technique or thinking strategy will yield the winning name. You just have to keep at it. And as much as I am loathe to admit it, when it comes time to pick the winning name, you may have to compromise: either the "perfect name" is unavailable, or despite your and your team's best efforts, you have not been able to find it.

But although you may have to compromise, it all might work out in the end. You may well discover that the name you at first didn't love, or that you felt was a compromise, grows on you. Industry lore has it that when the founders of Jet Blue were working through the naming process, they never were able to create a name they loved. Ultimately they settled on "Jet Blue," but they were definitely settling. And now, I'm guessing that they feel that "Jet Blue" is a great name for an airline and they couldn't imagine the airline being named anything else. "Only okay" names can evolve into great names as they become more familiar and build a history of positive associations and implied meaning.

Although the process is unpredictable, there are some tools and techniques—both mental strategies and group ideation techniques— that can increase your chances of success or at least keep you going creatively if you feel like giving up. All three process suggestions and techniques that follow fall under the heading of "think to the side" or "do the unexpected."

Picture Prompts or Collaging

The first suggestion is that instead of starting with words, use pictures to help you generate a new name. Since a name is made of words, it's natural to look to words for your solution. But the finiteness of words in the English language (or any other language for that matter) has a way of imposing limitations on the infinity of creative thought. Pictures can open up the mind to new creative possibilities, thinking strategies, and naming streams. In every naming session we do, we use either collaging or customized picture prompts to help generate new name possibilities.

Category Analogues

A second strategy is to use a version of category analogues to help create a name. You begin by identifying the key message, essence, or feeling you want your name to communicate. You're not naming yet; you're just getting examples of stimuli to help you ultimately get to your name. So, for instance, in a recent naming assignment of two new flavor varieties for a well-known gum, we decided that we wanted the name to communicate a feeling of fun. To create stimuli for an ideation session around this essence of fun, we did a short Survey Monkey survey of eighty of the company employees asking them to share with us things or experiences from their childhood and adult life that they considered fun: eating snow cones at the beach, raising their hands on the rapid descent of a rollercoaster, sacking the quarterback in a clutch situation, and others. We then used these associations of fun, giving each session participant more than a dozen examples of fun, to help trigger new flavor names. The naming session was extraordinary for the number of quality ideas stimulated in only ninety minutes by this simple and fun exercise. Of the more than one hundred names generated, twelve great names moved on to a quantitative test to help us choose the two winning names.

Tagline Triggers

The third surprising and somewhat counterintuitive naming technique or strategy is not to try immediately to name the product or service, but rather to come up with taglines for that product or service first, and then use the taglines as creative inspiration for the name. Headliner alternatives can help you generate these tagline triggers. A good example of this strategy was a naming assignment we did for Lutheran Society of America (LSA). The LSA is a collection of over 300 independent Lutheran health and human services organizations serving over three thousand communities and one in fifty Americans in the United States and the Caribbean. LSA had asked us to help it create a name for a new online auction service. The idea was that members of the organization could donate items to the Web site, and the items could then be auctioned off. It was an interesting, and ultimately very effective, member engagement and branding tool.

LSA had been feeling some naming pressure, which was partially relieved by having the creative session participants use expressions from the headliner program to help them create a tagline, instead of a name. Among the headliner trigger key words were *give, giving, good, gift, serve,* and *service.* Some of the winning taglines included these:

- Exchanging uncommon goods for the common good.
- A wealth of goods doing a wealth of good.
- The electronic yard sale that raises gift giving to a new level.
- Giving brought to a new e-level.
- Charity begins at our home page.
- The spirited auction place.
- The server on the computer is now you.

The tagline triggers exercise was a low-pressure way to free up the creativity of the session participants. Then we used the taglines as inspiration for the name. Among the names inspired by the taglines were these: the Spirited Exchange, the Giving Well, Trading Treasures, Grace Place, House of Cool Stuff, and the Giving Gallery. We then reworked and recombined these names, which eventually gave us the winning name: Trading Graces.

Ironically, after we had all agreed on the winning name, the president and CEO of LSA asked us if we would help them create a tagline for the new service. Their brief to us: "We think the tagline should say something about the nature of [the service] as a two-way exchange for mutual benefit and not convey a sense that it is the haves giving to the have-nots. In short [the service] invites people to be good neighbors." The tagline we came up with, literally overnight because of a deadline, was, "Trading Graces: Because everyone has something to give!"

Of course, not all creative challenges the facilitating leader faces are in the realm of new product creation. Far from it. It's to other business challenges, many not previously seen as within the purview of ideation sessions or creative teaming, that we now turn.

challenge: culture change

Key Strategy: Facilitating Genuine Employee Involvement

There is no tougher organizational challenge than changing a culture. Just ask any CEO or company president. Even the most powerful executive can feel surprisingly powerless when it comes to changing a well-entrenched corporate culture.

Nevertheless, my coworkers and I are occasionally called on to design and facilitate events to either launch a culture change initiative or help operationalize an initiative that is already underway. For the facilitating leader tasked with creating organization-wide change, the following example might provide some inspiration and encouragement as you travel down the challenging culture change road. As you'll see, the key insight or guiding principle in all the culture change work we do is this: involve those who are being asked to change to be a creative partner in the process of creating their own futures.

To increase the responsiveness, flexibility, efficiency, and effectiveness of its supply chain, IBM made the difficult decision to abandon its siloed approach to supply chain management, where each division oversaw the production and delivery of its own products and services. In its place, it sought to create an integrated supply chain that cut across all the product divisions. The result of this daring re-organization, initiated by IBM's CEO, Sam Palmisano, was that literally overnight, an IBM division, dubbed the Integrated Supply Chain (ISC) with $40 billion in annual spending with suppliers and nineteen thousand people, from clerks, to senior managers, to Ph.D. logistics experts, was formed in 2003. The immediate cultural challenge was how to move people out of their siloed thinking and identification with their previous IBM division and adopt a shared vision for the new cross-company ISC division.

It was only after mixed success with traditional culture change initiatives within IBM's supply chain group that we got the call from Tara Sexton, vice president of communications for the Integrated Supply Chain Division, saying that the team had decided it needed a more radical and creative approach. The challenge presented to us was, "Could we invent a program or approach that would help all of ISC's nineteen thousand employees achieve both a better understanding and, more important, a greater commitment to delivering on ISC's vision and its four strategic pillars?" As we later reframed and redefined the creative challenge, it became, "Could we help all their employees creatively operationalize ISC's new four-pillar strategy in their day-to-day jobs?"

Of course, this was a wonderful wish, but how could we possibly make this wish a reality, especially given the daunting numbers of employees? The solution my partner, Gary Fraser, our lead client, Tara, and I eventually came up with, after many joint creative strategy sessions, was to create a community of cross-functional evangelists to explain and, more important, facilitate every employee, directly or with the help of their coworkers, in a creative process to reinvent and redefine their roles and responsibilities within the new division.

After we did the math, the tactics of reaching everyone in the company were not that daunting. We built a train-the-trainer, trickle-down, creativity-training pyramid. At the top of the pyramid were our twenty-five creative evangelists. Each of them was responsible for conducting three or four four-hour workshops, with twenty-five to fifty senior managers and leaders in each workshop in various IBM locations around the world. In total, our twenty-five creative evangelists were able to personally train ISC's top twenty-two hundred senior leaders and managers.

Each of these twenty-two hundred leaders and senior managers in turn was tasked with conducting a two-hour workshop with his or her direct reports and coworkers. Ultimately, this meant that all of ISC's nineteen thousand employees took part in our four-hour or two-hour creative training workshop.

So why did IBM's supply chain leadership agree to this approach to launch its strategy rollout program, especially since it required such a significant commitment in terms of both employee time and company resources to implement? The key insight and driving principle behind Growth Engine's recommended approach was that to truly win the hearts and minds of all the employees at ISC, all employees should have the opportunity to reinvent, reimagine, and revision their jobs within the context of the new ISC vision and its strategic platforms. Gary, Tara, and I knew from IBM's internal pulse surveys that this was the missing ingredient in the culture change initiative. It wasn't that the employees weren't necessarily willing to change. It's just that they didn't know specifically how they were expected to change. The three of us felt strongly that it would be only after they had done this reinventing and reframing of their own jobs, and what they did on a daily basis, that they would be sufficiently equipped to both commit and make significant strategic contributions to the future success of the division.

Our proposed approach was somewhat of a culture shock for IBM's supply chain division, as it would be for any other well-run hierarchical, top-down, command-and-control organization. As Tara wrote to me in an e-mail,

> It was a bold step to even present this idea to the executive leadership team. Some of them would have been happy just to say we were going to make a set of charts and send them out to managers to take

employees through. And hard as I tried to avoid this perception, some thought I was suggesting these workshops would be to get people's opinion on the strategy. Finally, at the end of the meeting they realized, no, this is (as you said) to help create an environment that would allow us *to execute the strategy*!

We knew that the success of our proposed approach would be contingent on getting the right creative evangelists. These were the ideal criteria we set for these leaders:

- Comfortable leading large teams and speaking in public
- Previously identified as a high-potential, top talent manager
- Willingness and ability to commit ten days over a six-week period
- Geographically diverse group of facilitators for worldwide coverage
- Experience or expertise in more than one ISC functional area
- Conversant in ISC fundamentals, terminology, and strategy
- A willingness to team with local senior business managers to deliver workshops

Once we had identified these creative evangelists, we brought them to IBM's headquarters in Somers, New York, for a two-and-a-half-day train-the-trainer program. Our agenda included speeches by ISC's senior leaders to inspire our evangelists and help them understand how critically important their role would be in helping to build ISC's culture. Even more critical was teaching them how to facilitate their coworkers in reframing and rethinking their jobs within the context of ISC's strategic priorities. Because we knew that whatever we had the creative evangelists facilitate in their four-hour session would also have to be repeated in a simpler and shorter two-hour session for all the remaining ISC employees, we tried to keep our process simple. Ultimately we decided on a straightforward three-step process: envisioning the ISC future, barriers to this new future state, and cross-functional problem solving.

As workshop participants began envisioning the ISC future, we said to them, "Given the four strategic imperatives, imagine what ISC's ideal future might look like." And then to begin the process of helping each employee personalize this vision, we asked, "How would your world be different based on this new, ideal way of looking at the ISC?"

Next, we had the workshop participants work in table teams to identify some of the barriers to achieving this future state. And finally, we asked them to generate some cross-functional initiatives to overcome these barriers. Table teams were asked to be specific about these topics:

- How the functional groups could work better together to solve problems more efficiently
- How they as a team would get buy-in for their ideas
- What each member of the team could do to start to make this work

By every measure, this culture change and culture creation initiative was a huge success. Internal employee satisfaction measures (IBM's pulse survey) improved dramatically. Within two years, ISC achieved its cost-cutting, efficiency, time-to-market, and flexibility goals. And for the first time ever, more people wanted to work in supply chain than leave it because they could see how their day-to-day work translated to quarterly business results. The best indicator, though, was probably where people sat in meetings. At the beginning of the integration initiative, ISC's three hundred top managers sat with those from their own silo. At the end, they were sitting in cross-functional, process-oriented groups.

A great deal of credit for this outcome has to be given to both Tara Sexton and the supply chain division's senior management. For a company that specializes in technological solutions, to be willing to look beyond a technological fix (Webcasts, e-mails, video blogs, and so on) and commit to the time and expense of a very humanistic, person-to-person approach is impressive indeed.

This story also demonstrates the impact that involving employees in a way that encourages their creative contributions, especially when it affects them directly, can have on improving performance. Finally, it also highlights how critical it is to have dedicated and innovative facilitating leaders like Tara Sexton at a company, large or small.

challenge: sales forecasting

Key Strategy: Questioning Assumptions

One of the former Big Six accounting and consulting companies, working with one of the Big Three car companies, asked me to help them generate a more accurate sales forecast. The advantages of a better sales forecast were obvious: better inventory control, better use and allocation of company resources, and less price cutting and deal making to move fleets of overproduced, underpurchased vehicles, to name a few. All, of course, would lead to increased profitability for the car company, not to mention follow-up assignments for the consulting firm.

So why call an innovation and creativity consultant to help with a predominantly analytical exercise like sales forecasting? Beats me. I guess their reasoning was that since they'd succeeded in being creative and finding a better way in so many other areas of their business, they could also do it for sales forecasting. In theory, it was not a bad idea. But for me, who had to figure out how to do it, this was a daunting assignment.

Getting up to speed on the art and science of sales forecasting by speaking with executives from both the consulting company and the car company didn't help. Neither did all my prereading of *Harvard Business Review* articles on sales forecasting, inventory control, and supply chain management. If anything, this made me even more anxious. I couldn't imagine our creative solution being found in a better sales forecasting equation, simulation, or model.

When I am faced with a seemingly impossible task in the word of innovation, I know there are several ways out. One, which I call the Fantasy Island approach, is to wish for the impossible and then look for ways to make the impossible real. (*Fantasy Island*'s creator, Aaron Spelling, had an all-time favorite line: "Without dreams, there is no reality.")[1]

A second approach is what I'll call the Paul McCartney method. When the ex-Beatle finds himself faced with a seemingly impossible creative challenge, he often adopts what is to my mind a brilliant strategy: he gives up. By letting go of his attachment to a specific result that "solves the problem," my assumption is that he allows the problem itself to morph. The ultimate answer to his problem may lie not so much in solving it as it is in redefining the question. Put another way, it's the upfront assumptions that are being made about the problem that may make it seem impossible to solve. Apparently reasonable assumptions can lead to impossible, unsolvable problems and short-circuit potential breakthrough solutions. The key, then, is to take a step back and begin to question all of the assumptions you're using to define or frame the problem. One way to do that is to examine each of the words in your problem statement and then see if you can use another word or idea to help you see the problem in a different or possibly broader light. And that's exactly what we did with this Big Three car company in search of a better way to forecast its sales. Even more amazing, it worked.

To begin, I needed a problem or opportunity statement. I went for brevity and simplicity and came up with this: "How do we create a more effective sales forecast?" We then set about looking at the assumptions and creative possibilities in each word of the statement.

If we eliminate the sentence's setup words, *how* and *do,* we are left with seven words to consider. So, for instance, if we take the word *we,* what are the assumptions and creative possibilities inherent in or possibly implied by this word? *We* assumes that it is the marketing team that should be tasked with creating the sales forecast. But what if instead it was the dealers who created the sales forecast? Each quarter, estimates of projected sales from each dealer's selling area could be rolled up with all the other dealers' projections to create a national sales forecast. How about if consumers were responsible for creating the sales forecast? Could a sample of car owners be surveyed to see when and if they would be likely to buy their next car—and if that new car might be a Ford? This survey result might then be projectable to a national sales forecast number.

So which word do you think led to the breakthrough idea: *we, create, a, more, effective, sales,* or *forecast*? In fact, it was the least likely of all the words in the sentence that led to the breakthrough idea: the word *a.*

The group's eureka moment came when we realized that we had all assumed that there needed to be only one sales forecast. In retrospect, this was a perfectly logical assumption. After all, at the end of the day, there would be only one right answer: the actual number of vehicles sold. Wouldn't it make sense to try to predict the one correct answer? Yes and no. Certainly if we had a crystal ball, it would be wonderful to know what the actual sales were going to be.

Short of having a crystal ball, however, who says that we had to have the same sales forecast for manufacturing as we do for sales or the same forecast for finance as for marketing? After all, each department has different uses and ultimately different objectives for their sales forecast, and each has very different stakes in the outcome. In a Newtonian world, we'd all have the same sales forecast. But in today's world, where everything is relative, who says we all have to have the same sales forecast? The simple yet profound answer is that we don't.

Of course, at the end of the fiscal quarter, the different sales forecasts will need to be compared and even reconciled. But think of the learning that will come as each department is responsible for its own sales forecast, not to mention the time saved by each department not having to negotiate and ultimately agree on what they think the sales forecast should be.

I find it ironic that the key to unlocking a new approach to a discipline as sophisticated and complex as sales forecasting could lie in questioning the assumptions behind such a simple, one-letter word as *a* and its inherent assumption of "one."

What assumptions do the words carry that you are using to define your professional or personal challenges? It's something to think about.

challenge: growth strategizing

Key Technique: Positioning Continuums

We were working with a very successful discount clothing chain to create store-of-the-future concepts. To help prepare for the session, I looked at trends not only in retailing but in society as a whole. One of the things that struck me as I researched some of these trends was the dichotomies or complete contradictions that I was seeing in our country and the rest of the world. Yes, there was a trend toward eating healthier foods, but our society had never been fatter. Celebrities were hotter than ever before, but reality shows (at the time) were featuring everyday people. Being green was a major trend at the same time sales of SUVs were increasing. We were all time starved, yet spending records amounts of time on the Internet and social media. "Do-it-yourself" was gaining popularity at the same time as "do-it-for me" was on the rise.

It occurred to me that exploring what was driving these extremes might be a way to inspire very different, maybe even breakthrough new retailing concepts. What's more, we'd have two creative ways into the exercise: generate new store ideas that could reconcile these extremes or pick an extreme and build a store concept specifically around that extreme. The client wasn't sure how successful the technique would be (and, frankly, neither was I), but since it was only one of the five creative techniques I was planning for the day, they agreed to let me try it. The result was more successful than I ever could have imagined. At least a half-dozen truly revolutionary concepts for new stores came out of the technique.

And yet it wasn't because of the invention of this "dueling dichotomies" technique that I'm telling this story. It's that a potentially even more powerful and more broadly useful technique came out of this "experiment in extremes."

As I was facilitating the dueling dichotomies exercise, I found myself placing the extremes on either ends of a flip chart and drawing a line between these extremes to help the group visualize a spectrum or continuum of possible ideas. I was hoping that they would populate this continuum with a variety of new ideas between these two extremes. And they did. But as they did, I also realized that I had stumbled on a wonderful strategic tool: one that we have since used to generate ideas, insights, brand and company positionings, and ultimately strategic growth plans for both products and services—everything from detergents to bread, from a golf club to a design firm. We have even used the tool to help the human resource department of a luxury goods manufacturer do a better job of qualifying candidates and communicating their personal strengths to their prospective bosses.

We call this tool a *positioning continuum,* not because it's limited to helping position new products or services (although it certainly is a great positioning tool) but because it literally positions a product or service on a variety of strategic continuums. It allows you to see, literally, what place your brand or company occupies on a wide variety of continuums, while also comparing and contrasting your position on these continuums relative to your competition. (See Figure 5.1.)

Clients tell us that what makes the positioning continuums tool so powerful is that on one or two pages (depending on the number of continuums), they can get a clear, simple picture of where they are relative to their competition on the factors that matter to them most. And seeing where they are on these continuums at a moment in time also makes it easy for the strategic growth planning team to discuss if and how they might want to migrate toward or away from one factor or extreme to another. (Figure 5.2 shows directional arrows for these wished-for strategic changes.)

The positioning continuum tool is also interesting in that it is the process of identifying and creating the positioning continuum extremes that makes it such a valuable strategic planning exercise. What's in? What's out? What's important? What isn't? These are all important strategic discussions for the team to have.

Creating positioning continuums encourages the team to be creative about:

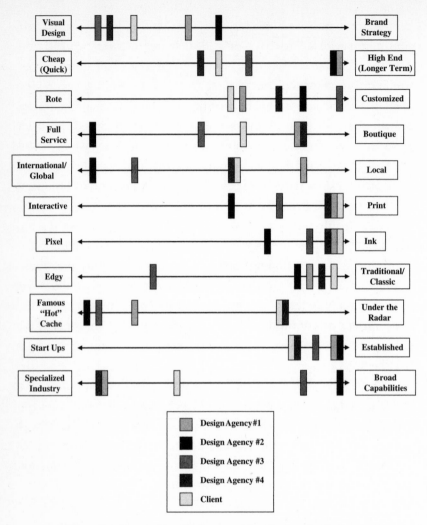

Figure 5.1 Competitive Environment Positioning Continuums

- Generating the diametrically opposed factors and extremes that make up the continuums. These factors are important because they help identify key benefits and drivers in a particular category or industry.
- Deciding where your brand or company should be placed on each continuum.

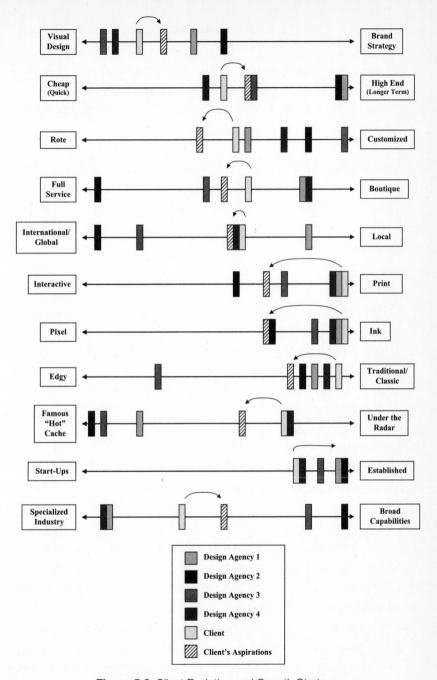

Figure 5.2 Client Evolution and Growth Strategy

- Agreeing on where your competitors might be placed on these continuums.
- Developing a robust and thoughtful strategic growth plan only after having considered where your brand (or company) is strong and weak relative to the competition, as well as identifying potential areas of opportunity or growth.

To facilitate this technique with your team, start by brainstorming lists of twelve to fifteen diametrically opposed factors or extremes. For example, if you are working on creating a positioning or developing a growth plan for a food product, your opposing factors and extremes might include these:

- Single use versus multiuse
- Preserved versus fresh
- Targeted to kids versus targeted to parents
- Healthy food versus junk food
- Delicious versus healthy
- Premium priced versus value priced
- Traditional versus trendy
- On-the-go versus at home
- Easy to prepare versus hard to prepare
- Great brand equity versus little or no brand equity
- Commodity versus differentiated

Then locate your brand or food product where you think it belongs on each continuum. Next, place one or more of your competitors on the same continuums. Finally, decide where you might want to migrate your brand or food product across these continuums to help you create a new positioning or strategic growth plan for your brand.

Two considerations as you build your brand, company, or service positionings are important. First, brainstorming the diametrically opposed factors and extremes is the most creative and important part of this exercise. Without relevant or compelling extremes, the exercise could prove less than valuable. Second, as the facilitator of this technique, you should not be overly concerned about placing your brand (and the competitor's brands) on the exact right spot on the continuums. Best guesses are fine. The true value of this technique lies in the discussions about your brand relative to other brands and where you might want to take your brand more so than getting the exact placements on the continuums.

challenge: group ideating without a group

Key Technique: The Whiteboard Technique

This final ideation and innovation technique is a tool that we created while working with a medium-sized manufacturing company, and we have subsequently shared it with many of our innovation clients. A wide variety of our clients have used this technique with tremendous success and without having to do much more than buy and post a few whiteboards around the office.

We were working with an industry-leading business-to-business manufacturing company that made parts for large printing presses. Our innovation process consulting work had been with senior executives, and the company's president gave us an interesting challenge: "What can you do to help me get more and better ideas from our guys on the line? These are hourly workers in our manufacturing plants, and we can't afford to take them off the line to do ideation sessions, but we still want their ideas. Any suggestions?"

"Let us think about it, and get back to you," was my quick response, not having a clue how we could help. My first thought was that this was an impossible request. The president wanted his workers' ideas but wouldn't, or couldn't, let them spend the time they needed to generate those ideas. Impossible, right?

But as I thought more about the president's challenge, I realized that although the workers couldn't use their time on the manufacturing line to be part of a group ideation session, they still had other time to think about and contribute ideas: during breaks, when they weren't on the job, or even when they were on the line, especially if they were in a repetitive factory job where they could conceivably be engaging in creative problem solving even as they worked.

The notion of creating some kind of suggestion box type of program for the workers was obvious but also made me nervous. With a few notable exceptions (such as Dart Industries, Toyota, and Frito-Lay), I knew that suggestion box programs have largely failed in U.S.-based industries and manufacturing plants. A suggestion box takes a tremendous commitment by a company to sell the program to get employee participation and, more important, follow up to vet every suggested idea. Both buy-in and follow-up are essential to make the program effective. Workers have to know that the time they spend thinking of business improvements will be taken seriously by their company. Without both a rigorous idea evaluation and an ongoing dialogue with the workers about the potential of and progress on their submitted idea, the number and quality of ideas suggested declines very quickly. I suspected that my client had neither the time nor the resources to create and manage an effective suggestion box program.

As I contemplated how to help this company create a program to generate new ideas, I discovered a wish I had: that the company's hourly workers experience the same energy and idea excitement that comes from group ideation as I had. Having run over fifty creative cost-cutting and new product improvement ideation sessions with factory workers in other companies, most notably for Unilever, I knew firsthand how exciting and productive these sessions can be.

I also realized that the problem with suggestion box programs is that not only are they devoid of this excitement of in-the-moment group sharing; they also lack the critical idea-building component that comes from a group ideation session. There was no mechanism that encouraged fair—or even good—suggestion box ideas to be built on or evolved by coworkers into better, even great, ideas. The ideas would all have to stand on their own without further creative input, so the chances of having a truly great idea come from a suggestion box were remote.

My creative challenge as I redefined it then became, "How do I create an interactive suggestion box where submitted ideas could be easily and efficiently built on by others?" My hope was that submitted ideas could get the extra attention they needed to grow and develop before having to survive on their own.

The simple solution that came out of this redefined creative challenge was a personal, team, departmental, or organization-wide interactive idea suggestion and idea building tool we call the *whiteboard technique*. The technique, unlike a traditional suggestion box program, is indeed interactive. It enables, and facilitates, the creation of more developed "big idea" ideas by promoting connection making and idea building between seemingly unrelated or random elements: thoughts, ideas, idea fragments, facts, insights, and intuitions. The technique allows workers to experience at least some of the energy, excitement, and concept productivity that comes from building ideas with a group—but without the physical presence of a group and without the organization having to devote planned or dedicated time and resources of a formal ideation session.

Here's how the whiteboard technique works:

Step 1: The manager (or anyone else, for the matter) who is looking for new ideas posts a blank whiteboard in her office or some appropriately public venue: a hallway outside her office, a break room, a conference room, near the water-cooler, the lunchroom, or even the company cafeteria.

Step 2: The manager decides on the specific topic or creative challenge for which she'd like her coworkers to generate new ideas and writes a short description of the challenge in the center of the whiteboard. The creative challenge could be anything—for example: "How do we improve productivity by 15 percent in this department?" or "What other new products could we offer?" or "How can we save money on our trade promotions?" or even an organizational human resource challenge like: "How do we make working here more fun?"

Step 3: Much like street musicians encouraging contributions by placing a few of their own dollars in their open instrument cases, the manager seeds the creative process by writing several idea starters on the whiteboard around the creative challenge. These seeds could be actual ideas or solutions to the challenge or fragments of ideas, relevant facts, provocative questions, wishes, potential areas to explore, or even ways to redefine the creative challenge.

Step 4: Write a time line at the bottom of the whiteboard, typically seven to fourteen days, depending on the nature of the topic or creative challenge. If you decide you want to work on the challenge for ten days, you list the numbers: "Day: 1 2 3 4 5 6 7 8 9 10" at the bottom of the whiteboard.

Step 5: Try to add something to the whiteboard each day and encourage your coworkers to do the same, no matter how seemingly insignificant, random, or trivial the thought, question, factoid, or idea might be.

Step 6: Each day, peruse the whiteboard, looking for connections and emergent ideas among all the seemingly random notes on the whiteboard. Write these ideas on the whiteboard wherever you can find the space.

Step 7: On each successive day, cross out a day on the time line to give the project a sense of urgency and impending closure.

Step 8: At the end of the allotted time, erase the creative challenge from the whiteboard after you have summarized and distributed (probably electronically) to your coworkers the ideas and other notes that came out of the exercise.

Step 9: Make sure something comes out of every whiteboard exercise you do. You must take some kind of action to demonstrate the value of participating in or contributing to the whiteboard technique. The action could be putting new product ideas in your new product development research and development process, creating a plan to implement a process improvement idea, or even a follow-up ideation session to develop and build on the ideas on the whiteboard.

Step 10: Select a new creative challenge to work on, and repeat the steps.

There's an important advantage that the whiteboard technique has over a traditional ideation session. Call it soak time, or the crossword puzzle effect (where the answer after "sleeping on it" can be obvious), the benefit of having the creative challenge posted for days or even weeks at a time, allows you and your coworkers to leverage the inherent pattern-finding, idea-combining, synergistic nature of the creative subconscious. You and your innovative whiteboarders may well discover that with this added creative "soak time," it'll be easy to make surprising, wonderful, and occasionally ingenious connections among the seemingly unrelated ideas and idea fragments randomly recorded on your whiteboard.

At the printing press parts manufacturing company, the technique yielded dramatic results almost immediately. The first time it was used was to address a manufacturing challenge with blanket cleaners, which are used to clean ink off printing presses. The ideas from a special task force of engineers had not solved the problem after several months of effort. Contrast this with the results from the guys on the shop floor: the whiteboard technique helped them generate two patentable solutions in fewer than ten days.

6

idea meets world
navigating the road from good idea to successful innovation

In the world of innovation, we know that ideas and concepts are very different. Think of an idea as the skeleton and a concept as a fully fleshed-out entity. Thus, as a facilitating leader, you're going to need to be creative about how you and your team flesh out an idea to turn it into a concept. In the world of new products, this means identifying or creating the product's unique benefits, positioning, name, package, product form, and ingredients. You can do this in an ideation session, and thanks to a request from a client, I've figured out a way to make it fun, too.

turning ideas into concepts: the billboard technique

I wasn't completely surprised when I got a call from a vice president of research and development from one of my clients looking for help with what he called a communication challenge. Over the years, this talented manager had assembled a team of top-flight team researchers and product developers. However, he was frustrated that his R&D super-stars were having trouble generating the enthusiasm and buy-in from marketing that he and they thought their ideas deserved. Could I some-how invent a technique, a process, or an approach that could help his team better communicate their great ideas to marketing, so that marketing would be as excited as they were about bringing their ideas to market?

I asked for a couple of weeks to think about it and promised to include whatever technique or exercise I came up with as part of a two-day innovation and creativity workshop I already had scheduled with his R&D department. After a few interviews with both marketing brand managers and the R&D scientists, I quickly realized that the problem was a communication problem: marketing and R&D were simply not speaking the same language.

R&D was enamored with new molecules, exotic ingredients, inno-vative product forms, and technically advanced dispensers. Marketing was trying to understand why any consumer would care about R&D's breakthroughs. The features of these breakthroughs would interest marketing only insofar as they could be directly linked to consumer benefits. Furthermore, if these consumer benefits could then be united seamlessly into one compelling consumer story, then R&D might really have something.

So the training objective and my creative process challenge became clear: create for R&D a process or creative technique that would enable them to present their ideas in consumer-directed, benefit-oriented language. I came up with several ideas, including having R&D write a print ad for their ideas, a TV commercial, and a radio spot. In the end, I decided on having them create the simplest form of consumer com-munication I could think of: a highway billboard.

Billboards may be one of the most underappreciated forms of pure communication we have, probably because they are such an environmental eyesore. But as an example of simple, clear, and concise communication, they are hard to beat. Creating a memora-ble and motivating ad that consumers have less than a second or two to see and understand as they speed by at sixty-plus miles an hour is not easy.

The simplicity and directness of the communication felt right for the R&D scientists and product developers. The billboard technique would enable me to train them in the basics of translating features into benefits without worrying that they might get lost in a process of wordsmithing, which they might if they were creating a print ad or thirty-second TV spot. The billboard should also be a lot of fun to create.

A highway billboard has three basic components: a headline, a visual, and a reason to believe (or call to action). Of these three, the headline was by far the most important component because it was the creative device that I was going to use to help them explicitly explore the consumer benefits of their R&D idea or breakthrough.

Here are the seven simple steps for creating a billboard:

Step 1: Form subteams of three to four participants each.

Step 2: Have each subteam agree on exactly the idea or creative breakthrough that they will be "billboarding."

Step 3: To help in this process of agreeing on the idea (and to help team members start thinking in consumer terms), give the idea a name. (Another option is to name the idea after you identify its consumer benefits.)

Step 4: List all the possible consumer benefits of the idea.

Step 5: Pick the single most important benefit of the idea, and create a short headline that communicates this benefit.

Step 6: Create a visual that helps communicate this key benefit.

Step 7: Create a reason to believe this key benefit.

As an example, let's say that R&D has invented a process that can encapsulate a skin care lotion inside an all-natural, flower-scented powder. Sprinkle the powder on your hands, rub your hands together, and the rubbing action causes the powder molecules to rupture, magically transforming the hand powder into a hand cream. It's a neat technology, but what's the benefit to the consumer? To billboard this idea, list some of the benefits:

1. Because this hand and body lotion starts as a powder, could it be less messy than a conventional hand and body lotion?
2. By starting as a powder before turning into a lotion, could it be much less greasy than other hand and body lotions?
3. Could the rubbing make the lotion penetrate deeper, and therefore somehow be better for your skin?
4. By magically changing from a powder to a lotion, might it make it easy for parents to get their kids to use a hand and body lotion simply because it's so much fun to use?
5. Could it provide a wonderful balance of hand and body moisturizing lotion with the silky feel of a powder, all in one product?
6. Is this the hand and body lotion that's best to use after you shower because it combines the drying properties of a powder with the moisturization of a lotion?

Looking over the benefits, especially benefit 5, a working name like "Silky Moisture" or "Moisture Silk" hand and body lotion might come to mind. If we then try to create headlines for some of the benefit areas, they could be these:

- Benefit headline for number 2: Moisture Silk: Pampering Your Skin Without that Greasy Feel
- Benefit headline for number 3: Moisture Silk: Because It Feels So Good Going on . . . and *into* Your Skin!
- Benefit headlines for number 4: Moisture Silk . . . Magically Transforms Itself, While Magically Moisturizing Your Child's Skin! Moisture Silk . . . Hand and Body Lotion Your Kids Will Love to Use!
- Benefit headline for number 5: Moisture Silk . . . Now There Are Two Ways to Pamper Your Skin, All in One Product!

Some of these benefits are more functional than others (pampering your skin without that greasy feeling, for example). Others are less explicit: "Now there are two ways to pamper your skin." None really focuses on a more emotional benefit. But all at least try to move beyond the mode of action (transforming from a powder to a lotion) to a true consumer benefit, which was what interested marketing. The billboard technique proved so successful as a concept development technique that we now use it in all our ideation sessions when we have time to do one or more rounds of concept-developing the highest-potential ideas.

the importance of insight

So you've just finished an ideation session. You and your team have generated 150 new ideas. The group votes and picks their 15 favorites. Of the 15, which is the big idea? Actually, who says there's only one big idea? Maybe there are a half-dozen big ideas. A dozen big ideas? How do you know? What separates a good idea from a great idea? You certainly think you know a big idea when you see one, but you decide to do the research just to be sure.

You and your innovation team write up the best concepts, hire a focus group moderator, and schedule time with target market consumers in a couple of cities. You make sure the focus group facility has sandwiches and pasta salad for lunch and sushi for dinner. Let the research begin.

Interestingly, anyone who has gone through this process knows that when you do start talking with consumers, things can change dramatically. An only okay idea can suddenly become a great idea while that best-thing-since-sliced-bread idea that you were so passionate about in the ideation session quickly turns into a hunk of stale dough.

How can this be? You know your business, and you have a good sense of the market. So what happened? How can things change so dramatically just by talking with a few people in Columbus, Ohio? Let's take a part-real (based on a brief conversation with a client), part-imagined example to get some insight into what can happen, and, as important, how (and what) you might be listening for as you're sitting behind the focus group mirror eating M&Ms or the occasional Twizzler.

Imagine for a moment that you are in charge of innovation for Pizza Hut. Five ideas came out of the ideation session you did last month that you're excited about testing in focus groups. At the last minute, you add a sixth idea, not because you think the idea's any good, but because you have the time—these are two-hour groups, and you think, *Why not?* Maybe you and your team will learn something that'll help you with another idea. The idea you add to the testing mix is one that's been kicking around Pizza Hut for several years and comes up in almost every ideation session: four mini-pizzas, all with different toppings, boxed in one large pizza box and sold for a price comparable to that of a single large pizza. You know from previous research that consumers like to get different toppings on each half of the pizza: some family members want pepperoni, others extra cheese. So why not double the number of choices from two to four?

It's not a bad idea, but it's not particularly creative and certainly not revolutionary. In addition, there might be some business issues associated with the idea. Will it be more work for the Pizza Hut store owners to prepare and cook four mini-pizzas versus one large one? And as a result, will profit margins go down? An even more important (and potentially disturbing) question might be: Will consumers be inclined to order fewer pizzas than they normally do because now at least four family members can get exactly what they want? What would your boss say about your launching a successful new product that reduced sales?

You decide to test the idea anyway.

So you do the focus groups, and it turns out in group after group, city after city, that this four-in-one pizza concept is testing far better than you ever expected. In fact, it's testing better than any of the other five ideas. It's beating the extra-cheese-in-the-crust concept;

the hot and spicy, low-calorie pizza wraps; and even the garlic-flavored mozzarella and tomato poppers. How could that be? A four-in-one pizza is a nice little idea, but certainly nothing to write the home office about. Or is it? What's going on here?

Could it be that this four-in-one pizza idea is about a lot more than just more different toppings? Yes. It's actually an ingenious solution to an important and pressing consumer need. It turns out that for many multimember families, ordering a pizza over the phone can be a real nightmare, sometimes even a knock-down, drag-out yelling and screaming match because two choices of toppings aren't enough. Some family members get what they want. Others don't. Or maybe nobody gets exactly what he or she wants. Everyone has to compromise. Either way, someone's disappointed or gets hurt feelings. I'm told from a client and marketing friend that this was confirmed by Pizza Hut when its marketing team "checked the tape." They listened to recorded calls from the Pizza Hut home-delivery lines from around the country and did indeed discover recurring and often quite intense family battles as the caller tried to negotiate a toppings compromise that would satisfy the whole family.

In fact, the importance of the four-in-one pizza concept isn't so much about four different pizza toppings as it is about having found a way to promote family harmony. That's an important insight and an example of how valuable focus group research can be when marketers are willing to move beyond listening for simple concept preferences ("concept A is scoring better than concept B") and rigorously probe the whys, wherefores, and the less-than-obvious motivations behind these preferences, especially in the early phases of the research. By continually asking: "Why?" "Why not?" "How come?" "Is that because?" and even, at times, "What if?" marketers are using focus groups for the greatest purpose: to discover true consumer insights.

Insights are so important because they can help you recognize an idea's true potential, as in the Pizza Hut example. An insight gets at the true consumer need that a product, in whatever form it's launched, is intended to address.

A consumer insight is also the key to effectively positioning and advertising the new product idea to consumers. In the case of advertising the four-in-one pizza concept for Pizza Hut, I had lunch one day with its former advertising agency creative director, Janet Lyons, who wrote the television commercial for Pizza Hut's four-in-one pizza. I had previously known of Janet's award-winning work for Pepsi but hadn't known she had also worked on the Pizza Hut business. And as we talked about the insight that led to the award–winning ad she wrote, with the Muppets fighting over which toppings they'd get, she confirmed that the insight about family harmony was indeed the key.

Finally, an insight can give you, the innovator, the confidence— and indeed the passion—you need to champion the idea within the organization and ultimately launch it successfully. When you know why consumers are so passionate about an idea, it can't help but make you passionate as well. And with this passion, it will be very hard, no matter what the internal political or production challenges, to talk you out of it.

So if insights are so powerful, how do you get one? Try ethnographic research.

Rubbermaid has its researchers shadow people as they do household chores. Moen videotapes consumers taking a shower. And we spent time "watching" in the restroom. It's all part of ethnography, a growing trend in research to conduct research not in some artificial environment (like a focus group facility, the mall, on the phone, or over the Internet) but rather in the environments where consumers are actually using products and services. The idea is that by watching, questioning, and interacting with consumers (or professionals) at the point of use, creative designers, researchers, and marketers will be able to identify shortcomings of existing products and identify new unmet needs that would never occur to them in a more artificial environment. The need and subsequent new product from Rubbermaid—a one-hand laundry basket (because so many people in a household are juggling so many things at once)—came out of ethnographic research. So did a new line of easy-to-replace designer shower handles from Moen.

We have used ethnographic research to help us invent, name, position, generate claims, and design packages for everything from oil filters to makeup, car wax to cereal bars, hair care products to bread. Whether it's conducting creative sandwich-making sessions at families' homes to test new lunch bread ideas, shopping the skin care and makeup aisles with middle-aged women in search of effective antiwrinkle cream claims, or conducting on-the-go video diary research with parents to test new snack concepts for kids, ethnographic methodologies can be as varied as the products and the environments in which they are purchased and used. We have also been creative about how to bring ethnographic methodologies into actual ideation sessions. Work with Unger Enterprises, a small, family-owned manufacturing company based in Bridgeport, Connecticut, is a good case in point.

Originally the manufacturers of only high-quality window washing tools for the professional market (think squeegees), Unger Enterprises has since expanded the business to include the manufacture and marketing of a wide variety of cleaning and maintenance tools (think mops and buckets) for professional and consumer markets. Like the other ideation sessions we have designed and facilitated for Unger, this one was well focused strategically with two very distinct cleaning and maintenance objectives: in the morning, generate new product ideas for restroom cleaning in buildings and industrial settings; in the afternoon, invent new products, both industrial and consumer, for cleaning in hard-to-reach, high-up places. As it turned out, it was the insight and idea in the morning that led to the breakthrough idea in the afternoon. And it was ethnographic research, during the ideation itself, that inspired them both.

Since no one in the ideation session knew much about cleaning restrooms in building and industrial settings, my ideation session design challenge was how to quickly ground everyone in professional restroom cleaning and still have enough time to generate new product ideas. Without at least some understanding of professional restroom cleaning, the ideation team might solve a nonexistent or unimportant problem; or, if we were lucky enough to ideate against a true professional restroom cleaning challenge, might not know enough to create a workable and truly worthwhile new product idea. And remember, we only had three and one-half hours for brainstorming restroom cleaning ideas. In the afternoon, we were ideating high-access cleaning new product ideas.

Could I have everyone clean a restroom before they came to the session? Possibly. How about if, at the ideation session itself, which we were holding at a Bridgeport, Connecticut, hotel, we had session participants take the time to clean a restroom? It's not a bad idea, but did we really have the time to do this? And could we learn enough, quickly enough, to help us ideate more successfully? More to the point, would anyone have a clue about how to clean a restroom? Maybe. But maybe not.

We needed to find someone who could educate us on a best practice of restroom cleaning. How about the restroom cleaning attendant at the hotel where we were running our session? Why couldn't he or she be our teacher? I contacted the hotel, and even though the manager was a bit taken aback initially by my request, eventually he agreed to let me talk to the restroom attendant and, if he agreed, hire him to help us with our ideation session.

The restroom attendant was young, maybe seventeen or eighteen years old, and of Hispanic descent. At first, I could tell he was a bit suspicious, and who could blame him? But because I assured him my request had been approved by the hotel manager, he was willing to listen to my proposal. After a little more explaining about what we were trying to accomplish and why, he agreed to help. And something told me—maybe because of the total lack of pretense—that he was going to be a great resource for us. As I finished the preinterview, I reminded him not to clean the restroom the morning of the ideation session. He promised he wouldn't. We were set.

The ideation session turned out to be one of the most memorable and satisfying of my career. To have fifteen senior executives, sales representatives, and designers hanging onto every word and action of a seventeen-year-old kid cleaning a restroom was for me a heartwarming example of how important everyone—no matter what their station in life—can be to the creative process. Admittedly, it couldn't have been easy for the attendant to have a bunch of "suits" crowding around him as he scrubbed toilets, washed sinks, and sprayed and wiped bathroom mirrors. But he was up to the challenge: very professional and, as it turned out, an excellent teacher. He did a superb job of patiently answering our questions while simultaneously doing the cleaning.

The breakthrough we were looking for came when we noticed he was balancing a variety of cleaning items as he was moving about the restroom: a cleaning brush, a spray bottle, a rag, and some paper towels. Since he couldn't get his large cleaning cart into the confined space of a restroom stall, he'd load himself up with what he needed from the cart and take them to where he wanted to clean. We also noticed he had an ingenious makeshift way of clipping the head of the spray bottle to his pants so his hands could be free to brush or wipe the sprayed surface. When we asked him what his wish would be for handling the spray bottle and other cleaning supplies, he said he'd love to have a cleaning belt that would hold everything he needed so he could do the job more quickly and easily.

The idea of a cleaning tool belt was not new to the world or even Unger. Unger at the time was marketing a simple nylon webbed belt to hold window washing tools. It also had a small clip-to-the-belt leather holster that could hold a squeegee. What was new were the insights about the belt. As we explored the idea of a professional cleaning tool belt with our seventeen-year-old expert, we realized three critically important things:

- A belt specifically designed for restroom cleaning would help the attendants do their job faster and more effectively. Better tools yield better results. Maybe the building's management could even save

some money as restroom attendants accomplished more in
less time.

- Entering this new market with a line of products would make this
easier for Unger. A cleaning tool system—anchored by a belt to
hold the appropriate cleaning tools—made it more likely it would
be able to sell in other, more traditional (some might say commod-
ity-like) products in the restroom cleaning line.

- Probably most important, we realized that a high-quality restroom
cleaning belt could elevate the perceived professionalism of the
restroom attendant's job—for the attendant, the building's management, and even the public. The belt could become a badge of
professionalism, reminiscent of other highly trained, tool-carrying,
working professionals (in the same way as carpenters have leather
tool belts).

It was the "professionalism" insight that led us to the idea of a
best practice training video or course. The idea was to produce a self-
contained training system (including a bilingual training video) for
restroom attendants that showed them how to clean restrooms effectively and efficiently, as well as gave management charts and checklists
for recording their progress. This was a very clever entrepreneurial idea
and strategy because the training video, which would be sold as a profitable new product, was also a means for funding the further research
and development of other new products in restroom and professional
cleaning. We felt pretty good that we ended up with two new product
ideas from one insight.

As it turned out, we still weren't done with our insight. In the afternoon ideation session focused on high-access cleaning, the group realized that the cleaning tool belt idea could be as important—and, as it
turned out, even more important—for high-access cleaners, including
professional window washers. Instead of a nylon webbed belt to hold
window washing tools or even a mini clip-to-the-belt leather holster to
hold a squeegee, we could design the world's best, most all-purpose,
easiest to-use, most efficient, and most professional window-washing

belt on the planet: a new line of high-premium belts Unger ultimately marketed under the name ErgoTec.

The late advertising legend Phil Dusenberry once said, "A good insight can fuel a thousand ideas, a thousand commercials."[1] It's been my experience that a good insight can also fuel dozens, if not hundreds, of new product ideas.

practical magic: three tricks of the successful innovator's trade

As innovation partners with our clients, we have a pragmatic view of innovation theory. Much of what we think and know about innovation has been shaped by the practical considerations of helping clients deliver, on an ongoing basis, innovation successes that directly contribute to top-line growth. We believe passionately in three innovation practices that we see validated over and over again in our innovation consulting work: involve everyone early and often, be optimistic and know there's an answer, and attend to the details.

Involve Everyone Early and Often

The two stories I share here about involving everyone early and often have to date yielded over $750 million in new sales.

Working with Thomas' English Muffins would mean, naturally, that one of our innovation challenges would be to invent new english muffin ideas. Sales of english muffins were flat, and indeed there was concern that the situation would only get worse, since it was older consumers who were Thomas' most enthusiastic supporters. New consumers would need to be attracted to the Thomas' English Muffin franchise for the continued long-term health of the business. Pete Rollins, vice president and general manager of Thomas', was our lead client, supported by brand manager Joe Morrissey. We knew from previous research that while consumers still love the taste of the only authentic "nooks-and-crannies" english muffin, they were also trying to have healthier diets. And so the obvious idea of how to make the "original" english muffin healthier became the focus of our work. A team ideation session, including senior management, marketing, R&D, manufacturing, sales, and even finance, helped us create a host of healthier english muffins. We elicited so many ideas, in fact, that the real question for our new english muffin product quickly became, "Healthier how?"

How about offering an organic english muffin? What about an all-natural english muffin? How about a whole-grain english muffin? Or even a "different-kinds-of-grains" english muffin? Who said an english muffin had to be made from white processed flour anyway? We began testing these ideas in focus groups.

In group after group, it quickly became apparent that the idea of an english muffin made out of healthier grains was the clear winner. Consumers loved everything about them. We even went so far as to pretend to denigrate the idea with consumers just to be sure we weren't fooling ourselves. Try as we might, consumers could not be talked out of them. They kept asking us when and where they could buy these new healthier-grain english muffins, always a good sign in a focus group. With budget approval from Thomas' parent company's board, we were going to launch the first new line of Thomas' English Muffins, Thomas' Hearty Grains. Honey Wheat, Oat Bran, and Multigrain were three of the products.

It also quickly became clear, however, that senior management wasn't nearly as excited about the idea as we were. Unlike Pete and Joe, Senior management hadn't had the advantage of sitting behind the glass and seeing and feeling the tremendous passion consumers had for this new idea. "Why not organic?" they asked. Organic baked goods were selling well in Canada. Wouldn't they sell well in the United States, too?

If not organic, they wondered, couldn't we start our foray into health by selling an "all-natural" english muffin? That way it wouldn't be such a radical departure from consumers' beloved "Original" white english muffin. If it were "all natural," it could still be white. Who'd ever heard of a brown english muffin anyway? Surely consumers would be put off by an "ugly brown English muffin," senior management thought.

And could R&D even make a brown, hearty grains english muffin? Keeping the famous Thomas' nooks and crannies with higher levels of unprocessed grains turned out to be a difficult manufacturing challenge. Interestingly, though, because R&D had also been part of the ideation and focus group, they had the same passion for the Hearty Grains product as we did. They assured us they would solve the manufacturing hurdles.

These are not easy decisions for senior managers. Thomas' Original English Muffin had over one hundred years of tradition—and high-margin sales. Was it worth the risk to try a brown english muffin? A failure with Hearty Grains could denigrate the entire Thomas' brand.

Have you ever heard the expression, "You can't steal second by keeping one of your feet on first?" Because Pete had seen with his own eyes the passion that consumers in the focus groups had for the Hearty Grains product, he was willing to jump in with both feet. His passion for the product carried the day with senior management, and ultimately Hearty Grains became not just a single-digit success. It was a rare new product grand slam. The Thomas' Hearty Grains line now accounts for over 30 percent of all Thomas' English Muffin sales and has attracted, as everyone hoped, an entirely new group of younger, more health-oriented consumers to the franchise.

Getting new products to market successfully requires vision, commitment, passion, and, most important, a dedicated (in every sense of the word) team. Without the help and support of everyone—senior management, marketing, sales, manufacturing, and even finance—from the start, it is doubtful Hearty Grains would ever have seen the light of the morning sun.

Another example of the importance of involving everyone early and often was a project we did for Danaher Tool Group and Sears that led to one of the most dramatic turnarounds I ever saw in a client.

Danaher Tool group, now called the Apex Tool Group after a merger with select tool companies from Cooper Industries, was (and still is) the manufacturer of the Craftsman line of ratchets, wrenches, and sockets for Sears. The Danaher Tool R&D team had developed a new product idea that was receiving little, if any, interest from Sears: use lasers to imprint much larger, easier-to-read sizes on the sides of the sockets. Dubbed the Hi-Viz socket, a 7/8 socket could now be read as a $\frac{7}{8}$ socket.

It's a nice idea, but it didn't seem destined to set the world on fire either. These Hi-Viz laser-etched sockets were considered an insignificant innovation relative to our larger project challenge of redesigning the entire line of ratchet, wrench, and socket tools, organizing and merchandising system for all thirty-four hundred Sears stores nationwide, and inventing new ratchet, wrench, and socket tool sets to help significantly expand the business.

To better understand current and potential consumers of ratchet, wrench, and socket sets, we conducted over forty hours of focus groups with a wide variety of target markets across the country. Among the target markets we interviewed and ideated new concepts with were heavy tool users, light and medium tool users, competitive tool buyers, women tool buyers, tuners (those who use tools to "trick out" their cars), and those who give ratchet, wrench, and socket sets as gifts. Ultimately our team's work led to a 10 percent increase in sales of Craftsman ratchet, wrench, and sockets sets and earned a record six vendor awards from Sears.

The work also had the unanticipated benefit of building a trusted relationship among the Sears buyer, the Danaher Tool Group sales and marketing people, the design firm (HMS design), and my company (Growth Engine). So the Sears buyer allowed us to test the Hi-Viz laser-etched socket concept, even though he wasn't sure the idea had much merit or potential.

It turned out the Hi-Viz socket was a big idea (both figuratively and literally) with consumers, who were more than willing to pay a 10 percent premium for it. Gift givers, for instance, immediately saw that those with poor eyesight would love the idea. "The perfect gift" was what some consumers called it. It went on to be a big success in the marketplace for Sears and Danaher Tool Group, even with its requisite premium price.

Because the Sears buyer had been willing to invest the time to be behind the glass, along with the rest of the new product development team, he saw firsthand the passion that consumers had for the product. And so, to his credit, even though he originally thought the Hi-Viz idea would not hold much interest for consumers, he was convinced and immediately approved the launch of the Hi-Viz sockets.

Had the buyer from Sears not been part of the process, it is doubtful that the Hi-Viz sockets would ever have been approved for launch. It's a good example of the importance of involving everyone, especially key decision makers, in the product development process. Of course, because of time constraints, the reality is that it's not always possible to have the key decision makers directly involved. It becomes even more important, then, to keep these key decision makers in the loop about the progress the team is making.

Know There's an Answer: Be Optimistic

It's easy to give up in the world of innovation. Invariably there will be obstacles that threaten to kill any given project. And for those less-than-committed innovators looking for an excuse as to why a project could not be made to work, there will be many, most of which will be entirely valid.

The true innovator sees obstacles not so much as project-killing roadblocks but as inevitable challenges to "doing the new." Consequently roadblocks are seen as creative challenges that need every bit as much innovative and creative problem–solving thinking as it took to create the original big idea. When a new product is being developed, for example, the hurdle could come from manufacturing constraints. Other times it might be the challenge of getting the price-to-value equation right. And still other times, the challenge could be more organizational.

We discovered an example of an organizational challenge and how it was creatively addressed when we were doing an internal innovation audit for one of our clients, Schick Razors. When we do an innovation audit, we generally are looking to discover two things. First, we want to find new product ideas: old or new or even past failures, consumer insights, unique manufacturing capabilities, trends—anything that can be the spark for an idea for a timely new product. We are also looking for innovation best practices that we could replicate with that client. To conduct the audit, we do individual interviews with sometimes dozens of employees in the organization, at all levels and in a wide variety of functions: senior marketers, brand managers, package designers, industrial designers, market researchers, manufacturing engineers, customer trade specialists, and others. Actually, "interview" is probably not an accurate description of what we're really doing. Yes, we're getting the facts as any interviewer might, but the exchanges are much more creative than that. Often they evolve into mini-brainstorming sessions. This is especially true when we talk with research scientists who, for instance, might mention the results of a little-known research study, or the "real reason" a product failed five years ago, or how, with the right study, the company could get a unique and ownable new product claim for a declining brand. A scientist might even have a pet project she started on her own, two years ago, for a breakthrough new product and is now sitting at the bottom of her desk drawer waiting for someone in marketing to champion its development.

The organization process suggestion for helping new products succeed at Schick came from interviews we conducted with an R&D scientist and a marketing person who together were responsible for one of Schick's most successful new product introductions in the past twenty years. The story is a great example of how important keeping a positive, can-do attitude is, both personally and organizationally, when doing new product innovation work.

Glennis Orloff, a new product scientist and engineer at Schick, came out of an internal ideation session with the idea to combine soap with a woman's shaver to make it a one-step, one-hand process. She made a prototype by hand that night and tried it the next morning. Somewhat to her surprise, it worked beautifully. Orloff then sought out marketing colleague Sharon DelValle to develop the idea into an integrated market proposition. Consumers were consulted on every element of the new product proposition: product design, ingredients, pricing, product positioning and communication, and package design. Of course, every new product development effort is a trial-and-error process. Unlike Orloff's prototype, getting things exactly right the first time rarely happens. And in the new product development process, getting all the elements to work together seamlessly, so that consumers are offered a new product with a unique and compelling benefit, communicated in a compelling way, at a price that makes sense is not easy.

Orloff and DelValle encountered creative challenges at every step of the development process, not the least of which was trying to secure a place in Schick's new product timetable and launch schedule. Many other new product concepts at the time were deemed more important, with potentially greater sales potential.

But Orloff and DelValle were clever about how they managed their idea internally. Every time they got a piece of good news about their developing concept, such as focus group results, manufacturing feasibility, or pricing, they shared it with the powers that be. When they got less-than-great news, they rethought, redesigned, repackaged, repositioned, or renamed the idea until they did. And because senior management had been kept in the loop, at least with all the good news, when an unexpected opening in the launch schedule appeared, it was an easy decision to approve the Intuition Razor for launch. And why not? It was the idea that "everyone had been hearing such great things about."

Attend to the Details

It's a great joy to work with clients who are passionate about their brand and the products they market under that brand. The Entenmann's baked goods company, based in Bay Shore, Long Island (and now owned by the world's largest baking company, Bimbo), is such a client. We have helped Entenmann's develop new products for more than six years, and it is still exciting for us to see how much they love their work and the new products that come out of this work.

On a recent new product assignment, we were helping them research a timely, on-trend new product idea: mini-cakes. As the name implies, these were single-serve cakes that, for the first time, made available Entenmann's most beloved cakes in convenient, individually wrapped packages. In-depth research, including home-use testing, told us that we had a winner. (And indeed we did: sales have been terrific.) As originally conceived, these were thin round-shaped cakes that looked much like a Thomas' toaster cake.

Consumers loved the idea and the shape, and we were ready to launch. But then the team had another idea. What if instead of trying to make the mini-cake look like a smaller version of a large round cake, we make it look as if it had been cut out of a square cake pan? So now the shape of the new Entenmann's Mini-Cake would be square instead of round. Would consumers care? Why even bother testing the new square shape? Consumers already told us they loved the idea in the round shape.

Successful innovation is about both keeping the big idea and big picture in mind while simultaneously attending to the details. If you lose sight of the big idea and what makes it unique, you may end up with a me-too product. If you're not attending to the details, chances are you'll have an idea that lacks integrity because all the pieces don't quite fit together. Consumers will then see it as a less-than-compelling proposition.

We decided to go that extra step and test the shapes against one another. We discovered that when the two cake forms were shown side by side, there was absolutely no question the square shape was preferred. The square Mini-Cakes cake "looked like a real piece of Entenmann's cake." The round cake? "Not so much."

Would Mini-Cakes have succeeded in the marketplace in a round format? Possibly. Was it worth testing the square shape? Yes. It took extra time and extra money, but in the end, it was worth it. It is immensely satisfying to know that we had all given our best to create a product that we love. Attending to the details was critical to delivering the best product we possibly could. In the end, it wasn't that hard going the extra step. You might even say it was a piece of cake.

■ ■ ■

Now that we've seen an assortment of thinking tools, ideation, and innovation processes to inspire creative breakthroughs for you and your team, it's time to consider these techniques holistically and understand how you might plan for and choreograph them in your team ideation sessions.

7

thinking like a
facilitating leader I
the who, where, and how of planning
and leading group ideation sessions

It is difficult, if not impossible, to dictate when truly magical things might happen in an ideation session. But some easily learned skills, mind-sets, and approaches to facilitation can dramatically affect a facilitator's effectiveness. Let's first look at the who and the where of ideation session planning, followed by a few simple and easily learned tips that can make your job as a facilitating leader that much more successful.

the who of ideation

Clients often ask me, "Who should I invite to an ideation session?" I usually give a three-part answer.

For stakeholders, I say, "Invite everyone on your team who'll be part of the execution [or funding] of the ideas generated in the session. Executing ideas is tough. You want people to feel that they were part of the process that created the ideas. Greater buy-in ownership means more motivation and commitment when you hit the inevitable organizational roadblocks when trying to implement your idea."

For creatives, I say, "Invite your most creative people." The client often responds, "What do you mean the 'most creative people'?" "Think about it," I retort. "You know who the most creative people are. It could be a secretary who's also a photographer, a market researcher who's writing a novel, the irreverent guy who's whispering snide remarks at deadly serious management meetings. You don't need a test to know who the most creative people are. You already know."

Finally, for wild cards, I say, "Invite people who both do and don't know much about your specific creative challenge and who don't particularly care about the session outcomes and deliverables and who know a little, or a lot, about a lot of other things. These are your all-important wild cards. As subject matter experts, they can provide valuable category expertise, trends, interesting facts, or insights for brainstorming fodder. Or as inherently creative people who don't yet know what can't be done, they can be the source of truly inspired, paradigm-shifting ideas. Internally, this could be people on other brands or from different departments. Externally, it could be people from your ad agency, promotion agency, digital, or direct marketing agency; editors from trade publications; or creative freelancers."

Over the years, I've worked with a wide variety of uniquely creative people in our ideation sessions. To give you a sense of the diversity of talent a session might include, here are six real-world examples of how we've used outside experts to liven up ideation sessions:

- The "Mayflower Madam" (Sydney Biddle Barrows) to help us invent a new perfume. As an expert on male–female relationships and a smart marketer, she was terrific.
- Tom Peters and Faith Popcorn to create a new program and philosophy for marketing to women. To my surprise, Tom and Faith, and a whole bunch of other famous and semifamous people, were great creative collaborators. One of the highlights of my work that

year was to see Tom and a facilitator friend of mine, Bob Taraschi, so excited about an idea they were creating together. Neither one of them could stop themselves from seemingly jumping around the room while making hand gestures to help visualize the evolving idea for each other.

- A half-dozen famous (in their world) dessert chefs to help us invent new confections for Godiva (the chefs were in New York for the Food Show). This group of international chefs also brought some of their original chocolate dessert creations, which could be described only as high art. The fact that we had literally several thousand dollars of samples of Godiva chocolate to snack on "as inspiration" didn't hurt.

- The beauty editor at *Jane* magazine helped us invent new cosmetics for Maybelline. It was she who inspired us to think about cosmetics, particularly for young people, in a whole new way.

- The *New York Times* architecture critic helped us invent the "retail store of the future for Bath and Body Works." His slide show of a walking tour he'd taken of New York the day before gave us an entirely new way to look at the world and, ultimately, store design.

- A half-dozen famous (in their worlds) inventors helped us invent the razor of the future for Schick. Specifically, we had a toy and game inventor, a tool inventor, an automotive inventor, a household devices inventor, a high-tech inventor, and a packaging/dispenser/ device inventor. Among them they had over one hundred patents. It was when one inventor began educating us about different ways to cut down a tree that we discovered a breakthrough idea.

Some of the more interesting experts I've ever worked with were not famous at all. In fact, as a group, they sound as if they come from a different planet, which for some of them wouldn't be far from wrong. Mensans are members of Mensa International, the high-IQ society that has more than 100,000 members worldwide. In the past ten years, I have designed and facilitated a wide variety of Mensan brainstorming sessions through LMCA, a brand extension and licensing company based in NYC. LMCA has an exclusive arrangement with Mensa International to use its members to generate brand licensing ideas for such clients as Honeywell, Roto-Rooter, Winchester, Ace Hardware, and Westinghouse.

Both the *New York Times* and the *Wall Street Journal* did stories on an LMCA licensing assignment ideation session I facilitated for Winnebago. When I started working with LMCA, I was skeptical that the Mensans would be any better at generating new product and licensing ideas than marketing people from inside the client company, outside experts, and creative freelancers.

As it turned out, the Mensans as a group weren't necessarily better than marketing people or creative freelancers, but they *were* different. And when it comes to generating new product and licensing ideas, in one sense, different is better. The client will take all the ideas it can get from wherever it can get them.

The Mensans are very smart people. The head of the New York chapter, for example, a plumber, has an IQ of 202. But honestly, most of the Mensans are not necessarily any smarter than the people I consult with every day in corporate America. I'm sure many of my clients (with a few notable exceptions) would pass the Mensan IQ test. So if it's not necessarily inherent intelligence that makes the Mensans and a Mensan brainstorming session different, what is it? I've come to believe there are four major differences. I share these not because I'm recommending you go out and run ideation sessions with Mensans. Rather, I think it'll give you some interesting ideas for how to think about and potentially change both the who and the how of your ideation sessions:

- As a rule, members of Mensa love to solve mental problems. Many of them also love playing with words and word constructions. So presenting your creative task as a kind of mental problem, linguistic or otherwise, can be highly motivating for some ideators.
- The variety and depth of hobbies, interests, and subject matter expertise is extraordinary with Mensa members. Want to know about the history of Etruscan pottery? Or how a Norden bombsite

actually worked? How to cook a catfish in an authentic Cajun style? Or ways to cheat at blackjack? There's a Mensan who knows. Obviously this breadth of knowledge and expertise can be very helpful in generating unique ideas and surprising creative connections in an ideation session.

- Since Mensans are all members of the same organization, there is a certain level of trust and intellectual camaraderie that is hard to duplicate with a group of strangers, creative freelancers, or even coworkers. As a result, Mensan ideation sessions almost always hit the ground running. To put it another way, the horse bolts out of the starting gate at the opening bell, and as the facilitator, it's sometimes all I can do to hang on. So in your world, in addition to continually looking for outsiders to keep your sessions fresh, it might also make sense to create a team of core ideators who, over time, can build up a similar level of mutual trust and intellectual camaraderie to the Mensans.

- The Mensans have no real investment in the ideation session. Since they are truly project outsiders, they feel little responsibility or pressure for the session to succeed. As such, they tend to be fairly relaxed in the session and don't overly edit their thoughts. And this willingness to say pretty much whatever comes to their minds is exactly what you want in a freewheeling ideation session.

I share some of the ideas that came out of a Mensan session for a specific LMCA client, Winnebago, because it'll give you a sense of the freewheeling nature of a well-run ideation session with intellectually curious freelancers. The purpose of the Winnebago session was to generate new product ideas and categories where Winnebago might license its name.

As an icebreaker, to play off Mensans' love of word games yet still be relevant to the task at hand, I asked each participant to pretend that he or she didn't know what a Winnebago was and then imagine what a Winnebago could be based on its presumed linguistic roots or its semantic construction and feel.

"Be creative," I said. "Could a Winnebago be a northern three-footed snow monster?" I asked as a way to prime their mental pumps. I had a hunch this word game puzzle would really get them going, and it did. Here are a few of their responses:

"I think of 'by the shores of Gitchee Gummee.' So I'm thinking a Winnebago is an Indian stud. I was just reading *Cosmopolitan*."
"It sounds like a prize you would win. Win a baygo."
"I thought of one of those big, old-fashioned woodie station wagons."
"The first thing I thought of was that a Winnebago was the second cousin to a rutabaga."

One of my favorites was the guy who actually whinnied the name *Winnebago* and said, "I thought it was a sound a horse might make."

We were off and running.

Here are some of the Winnebago licensing ideas that eventually came out of the session:

Hiking shoes	Water purification tablets for camping
Emergency road kits	Driver massage devices
Travel pillows	Mountain bikes
Baby strollers with all-terrain wheels	Expandable and foldable travel furniture
Scooters	Pet carriers
A national chain of rustic-motif motels	Road maps

Of course, the Mensans also came up with ideas like a Winnebago portable toilet and a Winnebago condom. Would it be fair to say that sometimes being willing to come up with stupid ideas is all part of the process of being smart? I think so.

the where of ideation

I used to think that where you held an ideation session didn't really matter. If you had a well-designed session with a variety of customized ideation techniques, combined with a team of motivated cross-functional ideators and a decent facilitator, the chances were very good that you'd have a highly productive ideation session. Indeed,

I've facilitated sessions where the environments were just terrible, either because the rooms were way too small or, worse, because they sent the wrong message, or "feel," for your ideation session. I'm thinking of a corporate ideation session I once had to facilitate in an old-style classroom, which included both a blackboard and those uncomfortable metal chairs, with the slab of fake, manufactured wood that (barely) fit over your legs so you'd have something to write on. I think the participants in that session were afraid that any minute, Sister Mary Joseph might come in and rap their knuckles for somehow misbehaving. I remember we once did an ideation session in a hotel that was so run down and poorly run that there was a large garbage bin directly outside our ideation room window with a huge rat on top having breakfast. It was not the ideal venues for sure, but even with these marginal environments, we still had very good ideation sessions.

So how important is the environment? There are two important questions to ask about the where of your ideation sessions. First, does the environment in any way limit the potential of your ideation session? For instance, if you are planning to do a triggered brainwalk, will there be enough wall space to put up your ideation stations? Or if you are forced to conduct your ideation session at the client's offices rather than off-site (not recommended), will people be constantly running off to check e-mails and not be giving your session the full attention and focus it deserves? At the very least, cell phones should be turned off in an ideation session.

The second question, on the positive side, is, "Could the environment in some way 'plus-up' the ideation session?" Maybe doing the ideation session in a beautiful or exotic location is a way to reward your coworkers or even inspire them to new growth possibilities for the business. Or maybe the environment provides a useful metaphor for your ideation session. I once facilitated a session for Coke to generate sponsorship and event ideas for the Winter Olympics. It was a lot of fun, and inspiring for the session participants, to do the session at a sports-related venue: Turner Field in Atlanta. The Atlanta Braves sports memorabilia didn't hurt either as parting gifts for the ideators.

The environment can also help you get outside ideators you wouldn't have access to otherwise. We've done sessions, for instance, for a variety of food clients at the Culinary Institute of America in Poughkeepsie, New York. We included the Institute's world-class chefs and younger, sometimes wildly creative, student chefs in our all-day ideation sessions there. We also had the delicious pleasure of having our lunch specially prepared and served to add further stimulus for our particular ideation challenge.

Finally, the environment itself can provide added ideation stimulus or even the raw material for a specific creative exercise. For instance, for a recent new product and strategic ideation session we did for Entenmann's, we held the ideation session in the wonderfully creative, boutique-filled section of New York City known as SoHo. As part of the session, we incorporated a creative "idea walk," which included stops at Eataly (the Italian restaurant bazaar), Restoration Hardware, a farmers' market, and a variety of bakeries and doughnut shops where session participants purchased products to use as thought starters for the afternoon ideation. Other stimuli-rich environments we have used have included the Maritime Center in Norwalk, Connecticut, to inspire claims for sun-tanning and sun-screening products, the Charlotte Motor Speedway to inspire new tool ideas, and the Children's Museum in our home town of Norwalk, Connecticut, to inspire new laundry product ideas for the whole family.

The point here is that the venue for your ideation, rather than in any way limiting you and your ideation team, can be an effective tool for inspiring you and your team to new creative heights.

more practical magic: seven tips for successful ideation facilitation

For many years, I was facilitating over a hundred ideation sessions a year. If you do the math, this averages to over two a week. Some weeks there were three sessions; a few weeks, there were four. The only time I did five in a week, I had a mystical experience on day 5 that is still, to this day, very difficult to explain. Maybe it was because I was tired from the travel. Or maybe I was energized by having facilitated over two hundred new ideas per day in four entirely different industries. It might even have been because I'd had four days of continuous and intense facilitator practice. But day 5 was quite an experience.

I can only describe it as a kind of Zen mastery moment of facilitating, where I was completely relaxed but also energized. I was entirely in the moment, ad-libbing funny but also relevant idea-evolving question prompts a split second after someone in the room proposed an idea. I was also simultaneously able to see and feel how even the most basic idea might find a place in the company's bigger picture and strategic growth objectives. It was the ultimate idea improv, with every soul in the room playing an important part in the flow of new ideas. I had the privilege and joy of leading this ecstatic dance of ideas without having, in any way, to be in charge. As extraordinary as this was, this is not that unique. An experienced facilitating leader would hope and frankly expect this to happen, often several times a day, in a well-facilitated, day-long ideation session. "Riding the idea wave," as I sometimes call it, an exciting and wonderful release of psychic energy and enthusiasm, often accompanies the creation of truly new and original ideas. But my experience on day 5 was way beyond even this.

To my complete and utter surprise, I found myself able to see, feel, and know the ideas that people were about to say *before* they said them. It was as if, for this very special moment in time, I was given a window into ideas of the future, a magical place where ideas already exist and are waiting for just the right time, place, and person through which to make themselves known. This clearly unexplainable experience lasted about thirty to forty-five minutes and has never happened since. To this day, I am still humbled by what I can only describe as an other-worldly, altered state.

I share this not because it's something I think ideation facilitators should aspire to. Indeed, I suspect that this was a once-in-a-lifetime experience for me. No, I share it because it is a good example of the kind of miracles that can happen when an ideation facilitator has given himself or herself so entirely over to a group, with a total lack of either self-consciousness, or the need for approval, that truly magical things can happen.

After over twenty years of facilitating ideation sessions, I've been able to distill my thoughts on the art and technique of facilitating down to seven, essential tips. They should serve you well as the facilitating leader of your team.

Tip #1: You Are There to Facilitate, Not to Scribe

The greatest challenge that new ideation facilitators have is to learn that writing down what's being said is secondary to actually facilitating and building ideas. The role of facilitators in any ideation session is to continually prompt session participants with interesting questions that either help dimensionalize partially formed ideas or idea starting points or inspire entirely new ideas. "Where else can we take that idea?" "How might it work?" "What other ideas does this make you think of?" "Where else might you take this idea to make it even better?" These are examples of the kinds of questions and probes that can help develop existing ideas or inspire entirely new ones.

If the facilitator spends all his time making sure he is getting the words down exactly right on the flip chart paper, there will be long silences while he is trying to capture what's being said. And not only will these long silences kill the group's energy and idea flow, it'll also mean that the facilitator will spend less time doing his job of prompting the group with provocative questions.

But you certainly need some kind of record. One option to capture ideas is to use a technographer, an electronic meeting note taker. In 90 percent of our ideation sessions, we have our technographer typing, in real time, the session notes on a laptop. Technographers are more than stenographers. They are capturing the essence of what's being said without including the extraneous verbiage that a word-for-word stenographer would record. The technographer then frees up the facilitator to facilitate the conception and evolution of ideas.

This does not mean that the facilitator shouldn't be writing anything down on the flip charts. It's important for the facilitator to write down key words, phrases, or short sentences that capture the essence of the idea on the flip charts. There are two reasons for this. First, if the technographer's computer crashes, you want to have at least some record, abbreviated though it might be, of the session's ideas. Second, and more important, it is psychologically important, and reinforcing for the individuals in the session, as well as the group as a whole, to see that their ideas are worthy of being captured.

Writing ideas down on flip chart paper also dramatically helps in the process of building on and occasionally inspiring entirely new ideas. For the group to be able to see the most recently facilitated two or three, or five or even ten ideas written across several flip charts at the front of the room makes it easy for them not only to remember these ideas but also possibly have them inspire (or combine with) other ideas.

Tip #2: Repeat the Idea

The other recording trick that I use when I'm facilitating is to immediately repeat the idea as I'm writing it down on the flip chart paper. Repeating the idea accomplishes three important things. First, it gives the facilitator time to write something (maybe a few key words to capture the essence of the idea) without having those long, energy-killing silences between ideas. Second, it becomes more likely that everyone in the room will have actually heard the idea, so that they will think about it, leading (we hope) someone else to build on that idea or come up with a new one inspired by that first one.

Repeating the idea also keeps you as the facilitator in control of the session. Since you're continually repeating what's being said, it seems natural then, if need be, to interrupt someone, especially if she is rambling, by saying something like, "Hold on. Let me get this down." "So what you're saying is . . ." "I got that you're saying this [as you write it down] . . . and you also said this . . . Does anyone else have a build on this?"

The final recording trick, which seems obvious but has important ancillary benefit, is to write very fast, even if your writing approaches the semi-illegible. Obviously writing fast helps you get more down in a shorter time. It also adds energy, pace, and excitement to the room, which is critical to keeping the ideas flowing.

As the facilitating leader, you're writing, repeating what's being said, thinking of the next idea-prompting question, and maybe even picking up nonverbal participant cues, all at the same time. An effective facilitator has to be able to operate at many levels simultaneously, both leading and being led by what's happening both inside himself or herself and around the room. It takes a tremendous amount of energy to do it well. If you're facilitating an all-day ideation session, expect to be totally exhausted at the end of the day. Only with practice should you hope to effectively facilitate two or, at most, three days in a row.

Tip #3: Don't Be Afraid to Bring Yourself

There's a misconception that being objective somehow means not being yourself. Consequently, some moderators and facilitators think that in the service of objectivity, they need to be emotionless automatons, fearful that if they let their personality show through, they'll somehow be influencing the ideas or biasing the research one way or the other. In fact, emotionless automatons influence the results, too, especially in ideation, and not in a good way. In ideation work, if you're overly objective (or as I think of it, "dead") chances are the session will be dead. Conversely, energy creates energy. If you feel excitement for an idea, let that excitement show. The group will appreciate seeing your honest reaction to a great idea.

Of course, if you let people see you're excited about a specific idea, aren't you sending the message that some ideas are better than others or even that some ideas aren't very good? Yes. There's a response I often hear in ideation sessions when someone says something negative about an idea: "There are no bad ideas." It's a well-intentioned prompt to "withhold judgment" in the spirit of Alex Osborne and brainstorming. But the reality is that most ideas are bad, or at least not very good. Typically only 10 percent to at most 40 percent of the ideas that come out of an ideation are worthy of further interest or development. And yes, it's true that we don't want to be negative in an ideation session and actually start criticizing someone's less-than-great (or even lousy) idea—especially since lousy ideas have a way of sometimes sparking a great idea. But that doesn't necessarily mean we can't or shouldn't show enthusiasm for a great idea. After all, if you're not excited about great ideas, why are you doing this work anyway?

The point here is that facilitators need to be authentic with the group. Being open gives permission to everyone in the group to be who they are, too. And as people feel freer to be more and more themselves, they are more likely to suggest risky or crazy, or funny or goofy things, and all of these can lead to the unexpected connections that make for a great new idea.

So don't be afraid to be yourself. Let your true personality show through. Admit your own limitations. Have fun. Make fun of yourself. Be excited by a great new idea. Laugh if you think something is funny. Don't laugh if it isn't. Ask stupid questions. Trust your gut. And even contribute your own ideas.

Tip #4: Contribute Your Own Ideas

The best ideation facilitators are creative and self-effacing, laugh easily, and are comfortable in their own skin. If you're a group manager or human resource executive trying to select employees for internal ideation facilitator training, using these simple, admittedly subjective criteria should serve you well.

The facilitator's inherent creative ability raises an interesting question: Should she volunteer her creative ideas in the actual ideation session? Every rule of brainstorming facilitation will say not to do this. The theory behind this "rule" is that the facilitator is there to facilitate, not propose her own ideas, which, rightly so, could be construed as competing with the group. But there are two solutions to the facilitator's "do-not-share-your-own-ideas" dilemma.

The simpler way for the facilitator to share an idea is to make a point of figuratively (and literally) stepping out of her role as facilitator. To do this, I usually say something like, "I'm going to stop being a facilitator for just a second and share an idea with you." Then I make a point of handing the marker I was recording ideas with to someone else, take one or two steps away from the flip chart, and then, and only then, share my idea. I use this facilitator trick sparingly—maybe once, at most twice, during a session. But it is a way for me to have fun with the group; I show that I'm in it with them and let them know that it's only natural for me to want to be part of the excitement of new idea creation. I am also sending the message (by calling out my idea contribution as an exception) that my primary role is to facilitate *their* ideas.

The easier way for the facilitator to contribute ideas—one that can dramatically add to the quality and number of ideas generated in the session—is to intentionally lead the group to create an idea that she has already thought of. She does this by asking leading questions that help the session participants to both recreate her original idea as well as generate other, often related ideas.

Again, asking leading questions makes it easy for the facilitator to share an idea without seemingly competing with the group or relinquishing her primary role and obligation to the group to act as a facilitator of their ideas. If she does a good job of asking leading questions, then no one will know that it was the facilitator's idea, and the group, instead of the facilitator, can take credit for the idea. That's okay. It's the facilitator's job to help the *group* generate as many great ideas as it can.

Here's an example of the kind of leading questions a facilitator might ask. Let's say you're facilitating an ideation session to invent new vacuum cleaners. Imagine that the group is in the midst of creating ideas for new kinds of robot vacuum cleaners. While facilitating these new robot ideas, you remember from your prereading, a focus group research report, that housewives and househusbands, when cleaning their kitchen floors, hate having to clean the floor twice: first to sweep up the dog hair or spilled cereal, then to wash and wax the floor.

The idea of an all-in-one, automatic kitchen floor vacuuming, steam-cleaning, washing, and waxing robot to address this "sweeping the floor twice" problem quickly comes to mind. So do a name and a benefit tagline: "Turn on the 'Night Maid' before you go to bed, and see your kitchen floor magically transformed from a dirty and scuffed-up mess at night, to a spotlessly clean, beautifully shined kitchen floor in the morning!"

Here are some leading question prompts the facilitator might ask to help the group invent his idea:

"You just created a new robot vacuum idea for the living room? What other rooms in the house could you use it in? The bathroom? The garage? The kitchen? Would you have to design it differently to work in these rooms? How so?"

"Is there anything that makes cleaning the kitchen floor different from, say, vacuuming a rug? How so?"

"You mentioned there are different steps in cleaning a kitchen floor. Is there any way to combine these steps to make it easier?"

"What's a wish you might have for cleaning, washing, and waxing your kitchen floor?"

"That's a great wish! Essentially, then, you'd go to bed at night with a dirty kitchen floor and wake up with a spotless and shiny kitchen floor. How could you actually make this happen?"

"So the robot would have to have four functions: a way to suck up and hold the debris, a water-heating chamber and delivery head for steam-cleaning the floor, a way to dispense floor wax, and finally a way to buff the wax. Is this right? Can anyone think of a way to make all that work in one simple and relatively small machine?"

"That sounds like a great design! What might we call this new device?"

"Magic Maid? That's good. Other names?"

"The Kitchenator! That's funny. Very good!"

"Any names that could capture the automatic 'set-it and forget' feature of this thing? Or maybe that it'll work at night so you don't have to."

"Nocturnal Transmission? That's funny, but I'm not sure that one's
   going to make it past the management committee."
"Night Helper? Night in Shiny Armor? Magic Night? Magic Knight?
   Night Shift? Night Nanny?"
"Night Nanny? That's great! Okay, let's move on to a new idea!"

So that's an example of how you might ask leading questions. Of
course, it begs the bigger question: Should the facilitator even be doing
this kind of leading? Aren't leading questions biasing? And isn't the
facilitator supposed to be objective? The answer is, "No, the facilitator
is not objective and in my opinion should not be."

Presumably the facilitator knows the kinds of ideas that will meet
the session objectives. As such, the facilitator should have a good
understanding of which ideas are in and which ideas are out: that is,
which ideas are wanted and doable and which are ideas that, for
whatever reason, are beyond the scope of this particular ideation
session. For instance, in facilitating a new product ideation session
for a new candy bar, you might know that there is one nonnegotiable
constraint: the structural packaging for the new candy bar cannot be
changed. The company has invested millions in its current manufacturing, and any new candy bar idea has to have a package that can be
run on the company's existing high-speed manufacturing lines. And
although you certainly won't call anyone out in the session for creating a new, different kind of structural package idea for a new candy
bar, you also won't spend the group's valuable ideation thinking time
to develop this idea further. You write the idea down and then
quickly move on.

Asking leading questions is an efficient and effective way for you as
a facilitating leader to help direct ideas without being overly directive.
You're at once setting the specific stage where the play of ideas will
happen but also allowing the freedom and creative space for new ideas
to happen within that particular theater of creative thought.

What if the freedom and creative space start to get out of hand and
you have someone who either rambles or starts sharing all the reasons

and rationales as to why his idea is great and in the process starts to have a negative effect on the group's energy and productivity? There are two fixes for this situation: the first can be shared at the beginning of the ideation session, and the second can be used repeatedly throughout the session.

To kick off an ideation session, the only rule I share is that unlike the rest of their professional lives, this is one of the few times where the session participants will not have to sell their ideas. As my partner and I say, "We are buying everything today, so no selling is needed." This is a subtle way to let everyone know that an ideation session is about coming up with ideas, not the rationales justifying them. Put another way, we're inviting their creative minds, not their analytical minds, to the session.

During the session itself, the best trick I know of to stop someone from rambling is to ask him or her to put the idea in a headline. The prompt, "Can you headline that idea for me?" is a good one because it presumes there's an idea somewhere in the ramblings. It creatively challenges the person to give a short summary of the idea, so that you can then quickly move on to ideas from others in the room and, in the process, keep the creative energy in the room rolling.

Tip #5: Name the Idea

You may have noticed in the robot vacuum cleaning example that the facilitator spent a fair amount of time getting the group to name the idea. This is an important and powerful tool for facilitating leaders to have in their bag of facilitating tricks. Naming an idea can give it focus, energy, excitement, and ultimately life. A name has a wonderful way of crystallizing the essence of an idea. Where the potential of an idea (and its consumer benefit) may not have been obvious before being named, it can be immediately obvious and often magically morph to a big idea with a clear consumer benefit after being named. For example, how excited would you be if, in an ideation session to generate new frozen meal ideas, someone had an idea for a line of lower-calorie dinners that tasted really good? Probably not very excited, right? But as soon as someone names the idea Lean Cuisine, that's a whole different story.

Finally, creating different names for an idea, as we did for the robot vacuum, might also give you very different ways of thinking about this same idea: a different target market, a unique positioning, or a nonobvious consumer benefit, any of which could help transform a mediocre idea into a great one.

Tip #6: Facilitate Deeper Than Broader

There are many ways to help evolve an idea, a fragment of an idea, or even just a starting point for an idea, into a concept: figuring out how the idea will actually work, understanding the idea's unique features and benefits, creating a tagline or naming the idea, being creative about the physical form a new product idea could take, or identifying its unique ingredients, package, or dispensing system. In the ideation facilitation work my company does for our clients, we have a strong bias that the facilitator should be facilitating deeper than broader. This means we would rather end a day of ideation with seventy-five to one hundred well-developed concepts than three hundred fragments of ideas. It's important that the group, encouraged by the facilitator, has the opportunity to dimensionalize the idea before moving on to another idea, for two reasons. First, it's hard to know if an idea is any good without creating or identifying some of the elements of the new product like its unique benefit, ingredients, or package. Second, and even more important, it's critical that the people in the room, who often have an intimate knowledge of the category (or categories) in which a new product must compete, be given the chance to share their expertise to help shape and improve a nascent idea. Otherwise, the talent in the room is not being leveraged to its fullest potential.

It's important that at least some idea building be done at the moment of the idea's creation: session participants are presumably in a state of creative thinking, building, and openness, and therefore creatively primed to do it. And despite everyone's best intentions, there most likely will not be time to do this critical building later. Naming the idea, quickly figuring out how it might work, and being creative about what would make the idea different from other ones already on the market are all quick, creative prompts that can help flesh out an idea without adversely affecting the creative flow of the session. Think of it this way: just as with the birth of a newborn baby, a new idea needs the immediate attention of its "parents" (and "idea doctors" in the room) to ensure that it will survive and grow.

Tip #7: Lose the "I"

This last facilitator tip is an important one for helping to facilitate an ideation session well, as well as for sending the message to the room that the session is about them, the people in the room, not you, the facilitator. As any truly great leader knows, you are there to serve your constituents and help them as individuals, as well as the group as a whole, to realize their creative potential.

The tip is very simple: lose the word *I* when you are facilitating. Not using *I* in the session is an easy way to ensure that you, as a facilitating leader, keep your attention on what matters most: the people in the room and the ideas that are being created.

Of course, losing the word *I* when you are facilitating doesn't mean losing yourself. Indeed, as the facilitating leader, you have to remain very much in control of the session. How do you reconcile the idea of being in control of the session with the apparently contradictory objective of creating an open, nonjudgmental environment where everyone feels free enough, and secure enough, to publicly propose risky, even crazy, ideas? The answer is paradoxical but simple: the facilitating leader must use the power of this role to ensure that a noncontrolling, nonjudgmental environment is created for everyone in the room. Therefore, he or she must not shy away from using authority as the appointed leader of the session to create an entirely democratic forum within the traditionally hierarchical, command-and-control structure of an organization. This person's job is to elicit the best ideas from everyone in the room, so if he or she occasionally has to keep someone from hijacking the session, particularly if it's a senior executive with a dominant personality, so be it.

■ ■ ■

Now that we've covered the who, the where, and the how of being a facilitating leader, let's look at a critical what: designing and facilitating a new product ideation session.

8

thinking like a
facilitating leader II
new product ideation session design

I magine that you have the luxury of bringing your team off-site for a
full day or even a day and a half of ideation. You have a variety of
ideation techniques you're considering for your session, but you're not
sure which techniques will work best for your particular creative challenge. You are also not sure how you should organize or choreograph
the techniques you do select throughout the one and a half days. So
what do you do?

For the purposes of illustrating the psychology of ideation session
design, this chapter assumes that you are facilitating a new product ideation session. Of course, the design strategies set out in this chapter are
applicable or adaptable to designing sessions for creative challenges
across the board.

We're going to pretend that we're facilitating a session to invent
new pens. Or if you prefer a broader category definition, let's say we're
inventing new writing instruments.

You've arranged to have a cross-functional group of ideators
at your session, including representatives from marketing, R&D,

manufacturing, and sales. Maybe you've even invited a few creative administrators or creative freelancers to round out the group that is now numbering twenty-two participants. You've got a great venue, with plenty of wall space for posting flip chart paper, and arranged to have round tables, or "islands," in the room. You've also arranged to have a technographer take meeting notes on a laptop. Logistically, you're ready to go.

It's a good idea to begin ideation session design work by generating a large list of possible techniques for the session, knowing full well that fewer than a third or even one-quarter of the techniques you list will make the final cut. Starting with such a large list of possible ideation techniques is reassuring for several reasons. With so many techniques to choose from, it's easy to start thinking about which ones might work best in a particular session. But it also begins to instill a level of confidence in you as a facilitating leader, knowing that you will have a wide variety of different and proven creative thinking techniques to help inspire breakthrough thinking from the session participants.

What criteria might help decide which techniques to pick? How will we customize the techniques we do pick specifically for inventing new writing instruments? And finally, how will we choreograph these techniques across the one and one-half days of the session? These are the three key questions that must be addressed to design a great session.

choosing techniques and drafting a schedule for the session

One rule of thumb that should guide the facilitator's choice of ideation techniques is a basic knowledge of the how-tos of facilitating the technique itself. Nothing will kill group energy faster, and adversely affect the amount and quality of ideas generated, than a facilitator who can't communicate the basics of how to do the technique. Session participants need to feel confident that they are being led through a series of creative exercises that can actually work by someone who knows what he or she is doing. A self-assured facilitator ultimately helps reassure the group that their sometimes unnerving excursion into this unknown world of as-yet-discovered ideas will be led by an experienced guide.

Assuming you know the basics of the technique—knowledge gained by either seeing someone else facilitate the technique, or by having experimented with the technique with a smaller group of supportive coworkers—what's your next consideration for choosing techniques? You might be surprised that I believe it should be the passion or excitement the facilitator has for a specific technique, or set of techniques. As you continue to facilitate your team, or even manage the person who is facilitating your team's ideation sessions, you will discover that some techniques work better for you and your team than others. And this can change over time. But because your passion for and confidence in facilitating a particular technique can so directly affect how successful that technique will be in the actual session, it's important that you feel good about the techniques you choose.

Different facilitators gravitate toward different techniques. This shouldn't surprise you since we all have different life experiences, personalities, and thinking styles. I, for instance, love the semantic intuition new product ideation technique (see Chapter Three). It's my favorite of the two dozen techniques we use in our new product ideation work. A good friend, facilitator Bob Taraschi, doesn't like it nearly as much as I do. Among his favorite new product techniques is target-market wishing. My partner, Gary Fraser, prefers questioning assumptions. The point is that there is no one best technique for a particular creative challenge. It often comes down to a matter of personal choice, preference, and passion. As the facilitating leader, you're the one who's ultimately responsible for the ideation session, so it's important that you pick the techniques that you feel will have the greatest likelihood of success.

Besides your passion for specific techniques, what other factors should you consider when making your creative technique choices? Here are some of the questions I always ask myself:

- Will the technique fit with the thinking styles of the people in the room?
- Can the technique be easily customized to the specific creative challenge?
- Can I find a place for the technique that makes sense in the overall flow of the session?
- What technique might add energy or fun to the session at a time when there might be an energy lull, say at 3:00 in the afternoon?
- Can the session location or room design accommodate the technique?

And most important:

- Will the techniques I choose, when taken as a whole, leverage and exploit the different creative capacities of the human brain? Put another way, have I included a sufficient variety of different kinds of creative techniques (questioning, metaphorical, visual, and fantasy techniques) in the session plan?

So let's get specific with these considerations in mind and design the one-and-a-half-day new product ideation session plan for writing instruments. You've looked at the list of new product ideation techniques (see Chapters Five and Six) and have some idea of which techniques you might want to include, but let's see how it goes as we work through the actual session plan and the psychology of the design.

First, a caveat and a few rules of thumb. In any ideation session design, you want to have more techniques planned than fewer. You never want to feel that you are stretching out an exercise just to fill time. But it's also important to understand that the session design should always be secondary to what's happening in the moment. If great ideas are flowing fast and fantastically, never stop the flow of these ideas just so you can "get back on plan." The point of the ideation session is to generate great new ideas, not do all the exercises. Think of the session plan as a kind of adventurer's road map. You may begin your journey following the map, but as you start to make interesting discoveries along the way, give yourself (and the group you're guiding) the time and freedom to explore these unexpected and exciting discoveries. That's the whole point of your trip, after all.

The important ideation session design principle here is that the facilitating leader needs to consider and be sensitive to the evolving creative mind-set of the group throughout the session. The session should have a natural progression, mental rhythm, and flow. Specifically, this means that the more left-brain analytical techniques (such as questioning assumptions) might appear earlier in the day and the more holistic, right-brain, or purely creative techniques (such as, say, semantic intuition) later in the day. The exception to this rule would be using a fantasy-oriented technique (such as wishing) as the first exercise to help session participants quickly move beyond the limitations of what they already know, to immediately start making new and creative connections.

Now let's see how these principles and considerations play out in our writing instruments session design.

new writing instruments: a day-and-a-half product ideation session

The day 1 session will start at 8:30 and end by 4:30 at the latest. People are fairly tired from a full day of ideation, so even 4:30 may be a little too late to end the session. We can see how it feels after we've designed it. Day 2 starts at 8:30 and finishes up by lunchtime.

You'll need to give all participants a prework assignment. You're not expecting that the prework will trigger any brilliant ideas. If it does, that would be great. But the real intent of the prework is simply to get people thinking about writing instruments before arriving at the session. The prework will get their subconscious minds working on the creative challenge well before they arrive, so that in the session itself, they will be primed to make some interesting creative connections.

Because everyone is so busy, the prework should be easy; otherwise people may not do it. What if you had them find a picture of where writing has occurred in an unusual or special place, say, graffiti, sky-writing; or a picture where they wish writing could be? So if they saw a picture of a rock in a magazine, it might make them think of a laser-etching, rock-writing pen. Or if they saw a picture of an ocean, they might imagine a writing instrument that enabled them to create messages that would float on the ocean surface. That would be fun! Having them bring pictures of places or situations where a new kind of writing instrument would help them record their thoughts in very different ways, possibly on very different surfaces, is sounding pretty good. It's easy, and you could see it generating some very different, potentially breakthrough ideas.

Day 1

Opening and Kickoff, 8:30–8:45

Someone, probably you as the facilitating leader (or possibly even someone senior to you), needs to give a brief background on goals for the session. This briefing should be general and upbeat. Too much detail, especially the history of ideas currently in the pipeline, tends to be counterproductive. Session participants might worry that they cannot invent anything nearly as good as any ideas they've just heard.

Icebreaker, 8:45–9:00

A great icebreaker does three things simultaneously: (1) it allows each person to introduce himself or herself to the rest of the group by sharing something personal, (2) it establishes and sends a message that this ideation session will be creative and fun, and (3) it gets people immediately into the ideation topic. If this were an ideation session to invent new hair care products, the icebreaker might be, "Tell us about the worst hair day you've ever had." For writing instruments, the icebreaker might be, "Tell us something creative, or fun, or even mischievous you did with a writing instrument when you were a child." If it's a very large session, with twenty-five to thirty people in the room, we might save time by asking everyone to share their childhood writing story with their table teammates and then pick the best story at their table for sharing with the group as a whole.

End-of-Session Excursion, 9:00–9:15

This is a quick but powerful projective technique I invented to help make everyone in the room feel both valued and unthreatened by the ideation session. Here's how a facilitating leader would describe it to the group:

> Imagine that it is now 11:30 tomorrow morning. We've just had an unbelievably great one and one-half days together. Incredibly productive, right? And really fun! So I'd like you to tell everyone what it was that you personally got out of these one and one-half days that you are most excited about. Remember that this is your personal goal, not the group goal or the business unit's goal. What did you personally get out of these one and one-half days that you are most excited about? And if you would, I'd like you to say it in the past tense: "So what I loved about this day and one-half was . . ."

We call this an end-of-session excursion exercise, and it's got a fair amount of psychology built into it. First, it establishes a success mentality at the outset. The technique presumes, by pretending to be at the end of the session, that we've already been successful. I once did a session for Minute Rice, and the people who walked into the room were anything but enthused. I asked the senior manager what was wrong, and he told me that the marketing team hadn't made their quarterly numbers. Everyone was a bit down, which of course is a tough way to begin an ideation session. So we did the end-of-session excursion technique, and although it started a bit slow, each successive end-of-session excursion got more and more positive. By the time we reached the last person, who said something like, "What I loved about this session was that I got several big ideas that I can take back to my team, and that I know will help grow the business!" the feeling in the room had shifted from one of failure to one of success. So, after less than ten minutes, we could be positive about Minute Rice.

Furthermore, by having each person talk about his or her personal goal for the session and not the business goal (although these could be one and the same, especially if you're leading the project), you acknowledge the different psychological needs of everyone in the room. This sends a message that each individual and his or her unique point of view is important to the success of the session. I've found that, ironically, the best and quickest way to bring a *group* together creatively is to begin by acknowledging each individual.

Wishing-Triggered Brainwalking, 9:15–10:00

We want to start the session with a technique that will get everyone, introverts and extroverts, involved right away. Brainwalking, our idea-volleyball technique, where everyone in the room will be writing down ideas at ideation stations around the room, before rotating to their neighbors' station to add more ideas, will certainly do this. Another advantage of brainwalking is that it is one of the few ideation techniques that can be easily combined with other ideation techniques. It's important to start the day with a success to help build the session participants' confidence in and acceptance of the overall process. Beginning with brainwalking and combining it with other ideation techniques increases the likelihood that we'll start the day successfully.

The question you have to answer in any ideation session design is this: "How can you get people very quickly thinking very different thoughts about a category that they may have been thinking about every day for the last twenty years—and do it in a way that feels both comfortable and easy?" The wishing technique, when combined with brainwalking, will do this. When facilitated correctly, wishing gives everyone in the room permission to think of fantastical, even entirely unrealistic thoughts. It's a wonderful way to start off without limitations, especially if the facilitating leader can get everyone wishing with childlike abandon. To help in the process, the facilitating leader can try to bring the adults back to their childhoods by saying, "Imagine that you're a three-year-old. Nothing was impossible then. And to help you think 'impossible' thoughts, I'd like you to intentionally create wishes that violate laws of nature."

As the group wishes for the impossible in writing instruments, the facilitator will be posting them at the brainwalking ideation stations around the room. To help prompt the wishing even further, the facilitator can have the group think of wishes for different kinds of people in different kinds of situations: "What would a truck driver wish for in a writing instrument? How about a runner? A baby? A toll collector? A stroke patient? A telemarketer? A lefty? An astronaut? A kid taking a test? A Department of Motor Vehicles employee? A security guard? A prescription-writing doctor? An ideation facilitator? A person from the future?"

Once the wishes are recorded around the room, the facilitator will divide the group into teams of two and have each team use these prompts as triggers to generate new writing instrument ideas at their individual idea stations. Then he'll have them rotate from their ideation station to their neighbor's ideation station and use what their neighbors wrote, or even the wishes at that particular ideation station, to trigger new ideas. Then he might have the teams rotate again, adding more ideas at each station each time they rotate.

On the next rotation, the facilitator could assign different trigger words, specifically verb modifiers, to each of the ideation station teams around the room. The verb modifiers technique uses the participial forms of verbs to prompt new ideas. Some examples of the more than two hundred verbs we might use in new product ideation include these:

accelerate	add	adjust	alternate
change form or shape	change lenses	change size	computerize
condense	crystallize	destabilize	dilute
disguise	divert	evaporate	evolve
exchange	flash on and off	go through a phase	grow
hybridize	invert	liquefy	measure
modulate	oxidize	pulsate	purge
purify	realign	rearrange	recombine
rotate	shed	shift position	shorten
shrink	substitute	swap	switch
synthesize	translate	transmute	transplant
tune	turn green	weaken	

Participants combine participial forms of these verbs (that is, -ed or –ing forms) with ideas already written down at their ideation station to create either a build or an entirely new idea. A pulsating pen? A "green(ed)" pen? An inverted/inverting pen? (That's the NASA pen.) A liquefied or liquid pen?

So that's it for the wishing-triggered brainwalk technique—almost. Let's listen in to the facilitator's instructions:

> As a final step, I'd like you and your teammate to rotate back to your original stations—yes, the ideation station where you wrote down your first ideas. Now circle any and all ideas you like. Yes, you can circle your own ideas. You were brilliant when we started this exercise, and you're still brilliant. You can circle as many ideas as you like. When we get back from the break, we'll talk about the ideas you circled and build on them together as a group.

Break, 10:00–10:15

Ninety minutes is about as long as you can go in an ideation session without taking a break. If you go beyond ninety minutes, especially in the morning, people will start leaving the room anyway.

Brainwalk Debriefing, 10:15–11:15

Debriefing the brainwalk is where facilitating leaders earn their money. It's their job to prompt the group to develop and build on the ideas circled on the ideation station sheets. Often what's written on the flip charts will only be a promising starting point.

The key facilitator tool for developing and building ideas is questions, lots of them, both specific and general. By asking the specific questions, you are trying to help the group move the beginning idea into a more fleshed-out concept (see Chapter Six). Examples of specific questions are, "How could that work?" "Any other ways to do this?" "What's a name for this idea?" "Who might this idea appeal to most, and in what way?" More general questions are designed to help trigger the group to a much broader view of the original idea, or possibly trigger an entirely new idea. Examples of more general questions could be: "Does this idea make you think of any other ideas?" "Could this idea be part of a larger platform of ideas? How so?" "Is there some other way, possibly in a very different form, to deliver on the benefit that this product offers?"

This in-the-moment questioning and facilitating makes it difficult to be precise on timing. We've allotted an hour to the brainwalk debriefing, but this may not be enough time. Sometimes a brainwalk debriefing can take up to two hours because great ideas just keep coming.

Prework Magazine Rip-and-Rap Exercise, 11:15–12:15

A technique to use after the wishing-triggered brainwalk could be the prework magazine rip-and-rap technique or questioning assumptions. There are good arguments for both. Questioning assumptions will open up the participants' minds to new possibilities very quickly. Personally I often like to wait until the end of the day before I introduce a visual technique like the magazine rip-and-rap exercise. This is because at that point, there has been so much creative thought given to the day's creative challenge, with participants' subconscious minds so primed with new possibilities and entirely comfortable with the process of making creative connections, that it's relatively easy for them to generate new ideas when they see a random visual. Say they see a picture of a rock star in a magazine; almost immediately, one participant comes up with an idea for an electronic, programmable pen that can draw temporary tattoos. Another participant yells out an idea for an "iPen," which stores and plays songs while doubling as a great writing instrument. Or something else. The group by then is riding the creative wave, and it's easy to come up with new ideas.

But if we wait until the end of the day to use the magazine rip-and-rap, we might have a bigger process problem. The prework may have stimulated some wonderful ideas that should be acknowledged and built on sooner rather than later. Otherwise the creators of these ideas might be preoccupied with finding "the perfect moment" to present their great idea and not be fully engaged in the creative process during the day.

So we'll go with the magazine rip-and-rap exercise in this slot. To vary the team makeup and facilitator dynamic (something a facilitating leader should be trying to do all day), we'll form teams of four, have them go to open spots on the wall, and ask them to post their prework pictures. We'll give each team a flip chart, and after they have agreed on a scribe, have them share with each other any ideas they came into the session with, as well as use the entire team's posted pictures to inspire new ideas. This should be a fairly rich and productive exercise, with each team typically generating six to ten ideas. Then have each team present its ideas to the group as a whole, encouraging the larger group to build on each team's presented ideas, before heading to lunch.

Lunch, 12:15–1:00

Participants have a buffet lunch, which will be waiting outside the door of the ideation room to save time.

Questioning Assumptions, 1:00–2:00

We frequently include questioning assumptions in the session plan because it is a highly productive technique, often leading to game-changing concepts for a new product. It is also a fairly analytical technique—at least, identifying the assumptions can be—so we want to do this technique early in the day with fresh minds, sometimes even before (or as a trigger for) the brainwalk technique. With the decision to start the day with the wishing-triggered brainwalk technique, followed by the magazine rip-and-rap technique in the late morning, though, we don't have much choice now except to put it right after lunch. But it must be right after lunch. Participants generally come back from lunch ready to work, so the analytical first part of this exercise, which requires energy, commitment, and a fresh mind, should still work well. If this exercise were placed in the midafternoon energy gully with tired minds, we'd be in real trouble.

Questioning assumptions is a three-step exercise, usually done by table teams. Each table team of five or six people is given a flip chart and asked to create a list of fifteen to twenty assumptions they're making about the product or category of products on which they're working. So, for example, in the world of pens or writing instruments, the list of assumptions might be:

My assumption is that a pen or writing instrument:
1. Is for writing something, usually on paper.
2. Is something you hold in your hand.
3. Is something you can write with more than once.
4. Has ink in it.
5. Takes physical effort to make it work.
6. Has writing fluid, ink, or something else that flows continuously and evenly out of it.
7. Has writing something as its main purpose.
8. Comes in different colors, sizes, and prices.
9. Will leak in my children's pants.
10. Cannot or does not know enough to be able to write things by itself.
11. Is portable.
12. Is not a computer.
13. Will eventually run out of ink or whatever else it's filled with.
14. Wasn't designed to interact with or be an essential part of my computer.
15. Is for humans to use.

As you can see, the variation and kinds of assumptions are broad indeed. Several assumptions are similar (for example, "portable" and "hold in your hand") but still different enough to inspire unique ideas.

Next, the teams work through the assumptions and use them as a stimulus to invent a new pen or writing instrument idea. Some ideas are obvious or easy to think of based on the assumption. For example, the assumption that a pen "will leak in my children's pants" leads directly to the idea of a pen guaranteed not to leak. Other assumptions require more work to turn into new ideas. The assumption that a writing instrument's main purpose is "for writing something" might inspire the team to think of other purposes for a pen and lead to a dual-use new product strategy. Could a pen also be a back scratcher, a laser pointer for presentations, a hearing aid, a parent monitor or GPS locator of kids, a tape recorder, or a toy?

In step 3, the teams present their ideas. As the ideas are being presented, ask if anyone has a build on a presented idea or even if a presented idea triggers an entirely new idea.

It's important for the facilitating leader of the questioning assumptions technique to know that this exercise is not about deciding on the validity (or falseness) of an assumption. Rather, the assumptions should be seen simply as stimuli for helping the team generate new ideas.

Patent Prompts or Worst Idea? 2:00–2:45

We have room left in the day for two creative exercises. We know we want to end the session with the semantic intuition technique for reasons I'll explain shortly. For this time slot, we're considering either patent prompts or worst idea. Each has distinct advantages and disadvantages.

The patent prompts technique (see Chapter Nine) uses abstracts of recently issued U.S. patents to trigger new ideas. We prepare for this by searching the U.S. patent database with key words and then using the preselected patents as thought prompts. It can stimulate wildly different, and occasionally great, ideas. Some of the search terms we might use to help locate the fifty to one hundred patent abstracts for the pen/ writing instrument session could include obvious key words like *pen, write, ink,* or *note.* But less obvious key words, like *record, communicate, draw,* or *message,* could provide the most interesting creative stimuli with the greatest potential for stimulating entirely new ways of thinking about the category.

Patent prompts is a powerful and effective technique. My concern, from an energy and group process standpoint, is that it is a two-step technique, starting with individuals working alone. Typically we give each participant three to five patent abstracts (no one in the room will have the same two abstracts) and ask them to select the one or two abstracts that they believe can help their team generate a new idea. It's an exercise that requires the ability to quickly see and transfer principles inherent in one invention to inspire a new invention. Some people are much better at this technique than others. And while patent prompts often leads to one to three truly breakthrough new concepts and is therefore worth doing, it is not a particularly exciting or energizing technique, especially at 2:30.

In contrast, the worst idea technique (see Chapter Three) is almost always a lot of fun, and it's also surprisingly productive. We'll sometimes include the worst idea technique in brainwalking, but it works equally well as a stand-alone technique.

Here's how to introduce the technique to the group:

I'd like us now to come up not with good ideas for a new writing instrument, but the worst ideas you can think of. These ideas could be gross, disgusting, illegal, sexually inappropriate— whatever you want, but they've got to be really bad ideas. If anyone doesn't like coming up with a really bad or disgusting idea, then feel free to come up with really stupid ideas instead: the kind of idea that if you were to propose to your boss, he'd think you were either an idiot or just plain nuts!

Since generating these worst ideas is a group activity, the facilitating leader can easily push the group to contribute really bad ideas. No one will take offense if you repeatedly say, "C'mon! Your idea's not bad enough. I want really awful ideas here!" This kind of prompt will make the exercise more fun, give everyone permission to laugh, and generate a welcome addition of afternoon entertainment and energy.

After the group has generated a list of twenty to thirty really bad ideas, spurred on by the facilitating leader to reach new lows of terribleness, absurdity, or idiocy, new subteams are formed that try to turn worst ideas into good, or even great, ideas. There are two basic strategies to do this. The first is obvious: "Do the opposite." The problems are that you don't always know what the opposite is, and the opposite typically isn't that interesting. The more interesting strategy usually is to say, "As bad as this idea is, what is it that I can take out of this idea or, better yet, what might this idea make me think of that I can turn into a good idea?"

Break, 2:45–3:00

It's time for a break so session participants will be reenergized for the last creative exercise of the day.

Semantic Intuition, 3:00–4:00

I often end a day of ideation with the semantic intuition technique because it's energizing and fun. And although participants are starting to feel mentally spent after a full day of ideating, semantic intuition has an uncanny way of enabling them to create entirely new, original, and useful ideas. Here's how the facilitating leader might set it up for the group:

> The last creative technique we'll be doing today is called semantic intuition. Even though it's got an odd name, it's a great technique for new product development. The way it works is that you name the idea first, and then you figure out what that idea is.
>
> Let me try that again: you create a name for an idea, and then, without knowing what that idea could be, you use the name you created to inspire you to think of a new idea. This is not as crazy as it might seem. There's actually a strong tradition of this in the creative arts. Songwriters, for instance, sometimes create the title of a song before they write it. It's true for dramatic writers as well. In his second autobiography, Neil Simon wrote that he got the name *The Odd Couple* before he wrote the play. Screenwriting legend William Goldman did

the same thing for one of his novels that was then made into a movie. He asked his younger daughter what she wanted him to write a story about. She said, "Princesses." He asked the older daughter what she wanted him to write a story about. She said, "A bride." He put them together, and we got *The Princess Bride*.

So that's what we're going to do with this technique as well: combine words to inspire new ideas. For writing instruments, we'll first have to create lists of words or phrases in three different categories. The three categories of words or phrases will be benefits of a writing instrument, features/functions/parts of a writing instrument, and verbs associated with a writing instrument. We'll divide the room into three teams, and I'll ask each team to create one of these lists of words on one of the flip charts. Do two columns of words on your piece of flip chart paper. This'll be fast. It shouldn't take you more than five or ten minutes to create your list. Go!"

Here's a sample of what each team might create:

- *Benefits of a writing instrument:* lasting impression, share a message, show your personality, compose an essay, portable recording, highlight things, immediately capture thoughts, a written record, personalized message, express things colorfully, inexpensive memory enhancer
- *Features/functions/parts of a writing instrument:* retractable head, pocket holder clip, long inkwell, thin shaft, finger friendly, easily held, thin line of ink, writes many/10,000 (?) words, personalizeable, sharable, spring action, promotional tool, brandable, steerable
- *Verbs and things associated with a writing instrument:* draw, record, write, sketch, trace, outline, personalize, paper, pocket holder, ink, colors, line thickness, permanent, nonpermanent, erasable, communicate, note, signature, documents, colorizing

When the lists are done, the facilitating leader might say something like this:

Now on to step 2. I'd like you to form teams of two. Pick somebody to work with you either don't know that well or haven't worked with today. Each team of two should have a writing instrument and a pad to write on.

Got your partner and your pad and instrument? Good. Now I'd like you to create six three-word or three-term combinations from the above lists, making sure you pick only one word or term from each list each time. For example your first three-word or three-term combinations could be "lasting impression" from list 1, "retractable head" from list 2, and "draw" from list 3.

Your second three-word or three-term combination might be "inexpensive memory enhancer" from list 1, "sharable" from list 2, and "trace" from list 3.

Continue making these random combinations until you have six triads. It's important that you pick words or terms that intrigue you in some way, but I don't want you to try and engineer the combinations. Making these combinations random is the whole point of this exercise. You're combining things you know in unknown or strange ways, which is a good way to think of the creative process. Do it quickly, and don't overthink it! You have only a few minutes to create your combinations.

Walk the room to make sure the pairs have completed their six triads, and then move on to the next step:

Step 3 is where this exercise gets very interesting. I'd like you now to use these six random combinations of words as thought starters to help you come up with two new ideas—ideas that we haven't heard yet today. So why did I have you make six combinations of words if you have to create only two new ideas? It's because some of these combinations probably won't work, right? They won't help you think of anything new. That's okay, and that's expected. That's why you have six combinations to create your two new ideas.

Let's do one together so you can see how this will work. If we take the combination: "inexpensive memory enhancer, sharable, trace," what new idea could this make you think of? Anyone have one? Before we talk about your ideas, it's important that you understand the goal here is not necessarily to use all three words. It doesn't matter if you use all three words or not. These word combinations are just thought starters. In other words, the idea police are not going to show up and say, "Wait a second! You didn't use all three of your words or terms." We don't care. Getting a great new idea—that's what's important. Okay, now let's hear an idea.

Let's say the idea you get is called "electronic tracing pen": it's a pen combined with a mini-camera and a mini-light projector. You repeat and summarize the idea for the group:

Here's how it would work. You'd take a picture of something, anything, you'd like to draw. Then the electronic tracing pen transfers an electronic replica of what you photographed to a mini-projector at the top of the pen. You'd detach the mini-projector from the pen, and place it on a piece of paper or whatever other surface you wanted to draw on. The mini-projector would project the electronic replica image of what you photographed across the paper so you could trace it. So the electronic tracing pen could be a great tool to teach someone how to draw. That's great—a fun idea.

This idea spurs an idea of your own, and, remembering that it's okay to bring yourself to the process, you say:

Actually I'm going to take off my facilitator hat for a minute and chime in. It occurs to me that this might make a great phone app. You might charge for it, but maybe you'd give it away as part of a promotion to promote sales of the company's traditional pen. "Buy twelve pens and get the Drawing Coach app free!"

All right! I'll step back to facilitator mode now. So does everyone get how to do this technique? I'm sure you noticed that the word *trace* became the key to this idea, closely followed by *memory enhancer* through the mechanism of a mini-camera. You could argue that *sharable* was a benefit of this idea since this invention indeed would be sharable, but the word itself had little, if any, role in inspiring the actual electronic tracing pen concept. We really used only two of the three words as triggers, and even at that, we morphed one of them along the way from memory enhancer to mini-camera. And that's okay.

That's the semantic intuition technique. It generally takes about thirty minutes to work through steps 1 to 3 and have the teams of two generate their two ideas. Then it's simply a matter of having each team present its ideas to the group as a whole and asking for builds.

Ending the Day's Session

After the semantic intuition debriefing, it's time to end the day. Thank everyone for staying with the process and for their ideas. Let them know that on day 2, they'll be selecting their fifteen to twenty favorite ideas from the printed technographer report. Then they'll have a chance to develop these ideas into concepts using a "fun concept development technique called billboarding."

Day 2

Idea Selection, 8:30–9:15

The technographer, the electronic meeting note taker, has printed out and made copies for each participant of all the ideas from day 1. She has numbered each idea to make it easier to identify and locate each idea. Your idea selection instructions to the group might sound like this:

Here is the printout of yesterday's ideas. As you'll see, you generated 287 new writing instrument ideas. I'd like you to go through the entire list of ideas and pick your top fifteen to twenty favorites. There are a couple of things to think about as you're making your choices. First, there will be repeats. Trish, our technographer, captured all the ideas from yesterday. This includes everything you wrote down at the ideation stations in the brainwalk exercise, but also the debriefing and building of those ideas, as well as new ideas from this exercise, which she captured and numbered separately. So vote for an idea you like only once. Also, you'll probably want to vote for a range of ideas: short-, medium-, and longer-term ideas. Take as much time as you need to select your winners.

I'll post numbered sheets at the front of the room, from 1 to 287. As soon as you have your top fifteen to twenty, go to the front of the room and put check marks next to the corresponding numbers. That way, we'll know immediately which ideas the group liked best.

Billboarding Concept Development Technique, Round 1, 9:15–10:30

If you allowed each participant to select fifteen to twenty ideas, there will most likely be thirty or so ideas that are the clear winners once all the votes have been recorded. If you have twenty people in your ideation session and you form teams of four, you can develop only five ideas in each round of concept development. So if you do two rounds of concept development, only ten of the thirty ideas will get developed.

You have two basic choices for deciding which ideas get developed: you (or the person who is ultimately responsible for the session output) can decide, or you can let the concept development teams pick the idea their team has the most passion for. If at all possible, let the teams pick the idea they have passion for to develop.

Here are the facilitating leader's instructions for the billboarding concept development technique (covered in some detail in Chapter Six):

We'll have time to do two rounds of concept development before we finish the session and have lunch. Let's form five teams of four participants each. Okay, now decide among your teammates which idea, of the thirty that were winners today, you want to develop as a concept. You'll probably want to decide pretty quickly because once a team has selected an idea, it's gone. So which idea does your team want?

Now that each team has its idea, I'd like you to create a billboard for it. This billboard should be one just like you might see on a highway. Usually these billboards have a short headline, a corresponding visual, and maybe even a reason to believe.

To help you create a billboard for your winning idea, first list all the benefits of the idea [to the consumer]. Then pick the most important benefit and create a headline that somehow highlights this most important benefit. Next, create a visual that helps explain or reinforce the headline. And finally, create a reason to believe for the headline and visual. For example, if you were going to create a billboard for Bounty paper towels, it might be:

- *Headline:* Bounty, the Quicker Picker Upper.
- *Visual:* Paper towel absorbing a spill.
- *Reason to believe:* Bounty has special ridged thirst pockets to soak up spills faster

You'll have forty-five minutes to create your billboard, and then we'll have each team present. Take your morning break any time you and your team want to.

Billboarding Concept Development Technique, Round 2, 10:30–11:30
Divide the group into new teams, have them select an idea from the top ideas that went unclaimed in the first round, and set them to developing five new ideas.

The result is that the writing instrument company will leave the session with ten well-developed concepts and another twenty high-potential concepts that the marketing and R&D teams can start to work on.

■ ■ ■

I have one last thing to share about designing and facilitating an ideation session: a big part of doing this work well is giving up control. Yes, you have invested the creative time, thought, and energy to select and choreograph the ideation session techniques your experience and intuition tell you will have the greatest likelihood of success. But there's only so much you can control when the sessions start and the ideas begin to come. At its essence, this work is improvisation. And what makes improvisation so scary, fun, and wonderful, all at the same time, is the in-the-moment surprises and unexpected connections. And that, of course, is what being truly creative is about.

9

thinking like a
facilitating leader III
five strategies for inventing ideation and innovation processes

Every ideation session is different and every innovation challenge unique. And while I fully expect that the ideation techniques and innovation processes in this book will serve you well for the majority of your challenges as a creative facilitating leader, there are times when you will want or need to invent your own creative techniques, processes, and approaches. What follows are the five thinking strategies that I use to invent new creative techniques for unique or unanticipated (or both) business challenges:

- Matching like-to-like stimuli
- Going to extremes
- Thinking of the 5 Ws
- Combining techniques
- Creating a success footprint

matching like-to-like stimuli

A number of firms do worldwide searches of new products. Mintel, the one we use most often on behalf of our clients, is the best. Companies retain Mintel to provide them with reports identifying new products that have been introduced around the world in their particular categories of products. It's a powerful competitive intelligence and trend tool and an invaluable ideation tool.

Three of my coworkers from Growth Engine and I had been asked to facilitate a two-day ideation session with forty-five senior marketers and research and development executives at a leading skin care company. We organized the two days around different skin care conditions or categories: dry skin, acne, sun care, and antiaging. We built exercises that were designed to generate ideas in each of these categories. And we also built exercises to generate ideas across categories. In both cases we used products from around the world, provided by Mintel, as stimulus for the session. So, for instance, in the acne category, we have pictures of products that list their ingredients and claims. How could you not come up with a new acne product idea when you see products with names like these?

- "No Zit Sherlock Breakout Busting Rubberizing Mask" by Bliss
- "Yes to Tomatoes Clear Skin Deep Cleansing Facial Pads" (from France)
- Soap and Glory's "Scrub Your Nose in It Multitasking Scrub and Mask" (from Norway)
- "Venom Essence" by A. C. Care (in Japan), which uses bee venom as an antibacterial
- "Blackhead Blitzer" face tonic mask (from Thailand)
- "Skin Fruits" from Indonesia, or "Ice Fruits" from Malaysia, or "Soda" (a baking soda pore cleansing foam from South Korea)

The worst-case scenario is that prompts like these should inspire you and your team to say, "Well, at least we can do better than some of these products that are already on the market!"

That is an example of how we'll use the principle of like-to-like and the tool of global product research as stimuli for new product ideation. The stimuli can be sourced from anywhere, and this sort of technique can be adapted to countless business challenges. What is important when using like-to-like stimuli in an ideation technique is that participants be encouraged to adopt the principle-finding and principle-transfer creative mind-set (see Chapter One). The stimuli are not intended to give you an idea. Rather, they should be seen as thought starters, inspiring you and your team to create and pursue ideas you otherwise might not have. In the acne example, for instance, using bee venom as an antibacterial face wash is intriguing. The success of Botox in wrinkle removing and (apparently) bee venom in acne makes one wonder if a whole class of toxic substances could be used effectively in a wide variety of skin care treatments. What about using snake venom to open up pores or the poison in blowfish to kill bacteria deep in the skin? Who knows if they would work? But they're interesting territories to explore, which is exactly the point.

Consider how you might use the like-to-like strategy for inventing new products and services in, say, the financial services industry. I addressed just such a creative process challenge for one of the large accounting firms. The like-to-like exercise I created for our ideation session for new financial services was to have the participants read the financial sections of both the *New York Times* and the *Wall Street Journal* with a creative eye: looking for problems, unmet needs, and interesting challenges confronting the financial services industry. This financial page news scan technique was quite effective. One idea that came out of it was a one-stop service for recruiting, training, advising, and insuring current and future members of the boards of directors of medium- and large-sized companies.

In another instance, a strategy session for a large information services company, we were asked to ideate new business growth models for the company. And so I created a like-to-like information business model exercise, using Web page screenshots detailing little-known or unique services from well-known information companies as thought starters and prompts. Among the more than twenty-five organizations with unique information services and business models we profiled and used as prompts were Match.com, CNBC, Wikipedia, Craigslist, Amazon, FedEx, the U.S. Postal Service, and the Internal Revenue Service.

If you're trying to invent a new food product, two of the like-to-like exercises you might try using are cookbooks or recipes as creative prompts or using menus from around the world to trigger new ideas. Obvious, right? But what if you were looking for creative ways to defend a patent or even creative ways to invent around a patent? I was asked to design a patent defense creative session for a Fortune 500 automotive parts firm. The idea was to focus the session on one of its existing patents and, as a way to defend it, invent as many ways around this patent as we possibly could. The company could then patent these other ideas before the competition did, essentially locking out the others from an intellectual property option or advantage.

In this case, one of the like-to-like techniques I used in the session was one I had come up with several years earlier for the same company to help it invent new automotive hoses—a like-to-like invention technique. The technique I created is called patent prompts. Now that the U.S. Patent and Trademark office has put all of its more than 8 million issued patents online, patents can be searched electronically using key words. For instance, if you were looking for stimuli to trigger new automotive hose ideas, you might enter an obvious key word like *hose* into your search. More than ninety-five thousand patents containing the word *hose* somewhere in the write-up of the patent would be returned from your free online search. As you work through the patent abstracts of some of these patents, you could print out, and use as stimuli in your ideation session, the patent abstracts that you think might trigger an interesting new automotive hose idea from the session participants. For instance, patent number 8,015,659 is for "an airflow passage for a vacuum cleaner." Patent number 8,011,059 is for a "low-profile air duct fitting for passage of air through narrow openings and method of using the same." And patent number 8,012,141 is for a "suction wand" that includes "a pressable button or similar device for allowing a user to regulate suction through the suction wand."

The objective in using these patent abstracts is not necessarily to invent ways to circumvent a particular patent; rather, it is a way to stimulate your ideation team to think of new ideas by transferring the inherent principle, mechanism, or feature of a patented idea to their unique creative challenge. Although this could be thought of as a like-to-like technique, it does not have to be limited to close-in hose ideas. Your patent search could include words like *flow, air, transfer,* or *channel* or any of a hundred other key words that might reflect what an air hose does—or what you might wish it could do.

Does the patent prompts technique work best with technically trained session participants? We have certainly used it successfully with Ph.D. scientists and engineers to invent everything from new fuse boxes to roof shingles. But we have also used it every bit as successfully with average session participants, helping to inspire them to invent new hair care products, toys, and envelopes.

So whether it's patents, cookbooks, or financial articles from the *New York Times*, at its essence, the like-to-like thinking strategy is about finding stimuli that are somehow related to the creative task you're addressing but also different enough to stimulate new thinking.

going to extremes

A focused ideation technique I often use to start an ideation session to make sure that we're tuning into consumer wants, needs, and wishes is one we call target market wishing. We have session participants identify different target markets and then imagine what these target markets might wish for. As an example, when we were trying to creatively solve what even our client said was "an impossible challenge"—selling an expensive U.S. antipsychotic drug to eastern European governments and health organizations—it was the target market wishing technique that ultimately provided the breakthrough marketing ideas. Which target markets would be relevent to government or health officials who purchase anti-psychotic prescription drugs? Nurses? Patients? Family members of the schizophrenic patients? Psychiatrists? Employers of the patients? Friends of the patients? Legislators? Hospital administrators? Role-playing these target markets made it easier for session participants to wish for the impossible since it "wasn't them" doing the wishing; it was the person they were role-playing. One of the most exciting selling solutions came from role-playing a government purchasing agent who, when he looked at the bigger picture of the costs to society associated with not approving the purchase of the drug, realized it made a great deal of sense to approve the drug. As the president of this pharmaceutical division told his team on completion of the project: "You truly succeeded in doing the impossible." Such is the power of wishing!

The wishing technique, if it's being facilitated correctly, pushes one's thinking to the extremes. In its creative essence, it is about wishing for the impossible. But could the technique itself be pushed even further and be made even more extreme? What could be more extreme than the impossible?

Although the target market wishing technique encourages wishing for the impossible, it still has a basis in reality because the target markets that are being role-played are real. Pushing the real to the unreal presents an opportunity to help session participants to be even more fantastical in their thinking. And fantastical thinking can be especially valuable in new product work, where, after years or even decades of working in a particular category, the ideation team may need to be quickly jolted out of their conventional creative thinking strategies.

A good example of pushing the target market wishing technique to a fantastical extreme was a new product development ideation session I did for Estée Lauder and its Prescriptives brand. Our goal was to create a breakthrough new makeup concept, and so I had the group enter the world of the fantastical by imagining the makeup needs of more than a dozen very unreal target markets. These included mummies, mermaids, a race of people from the Rainbow Sun Planet (the sun changes its color every day), chameleon people, snake people (they take their skin off at night and put it back on in the morning), space shuttle tiles skin people, wax people, mirror people (they have patches of reflective skin all over their body), antismoke people (their skin is allergic to smoke), animated characters, and vampires.

What kind of makeup might a mermaid need? Would she have chronically water-damaged skin that would need to be compensated for in a makeup? Or would the makeup simply need to be waterproof? Might the makeup be formulated to bond with the minerals in the seawater to give the skin a special all-natural, healthy glow?

What would an animated character wish for in a makeup? A way to make its skin look less two-dimensional? How about a way to leverage the light coming through the character's "animated" face?

It was this fantasy target market wishing exercise that led to the aptly titled and highly successful new line of makeup called Magic. The revolutionary new product concept was a line of makeup made with light-reflecting properties to help reduce the appearance of wrinkles while simultaneously giving the skin a glowing, more vibrant look and feel.

To create your own going-to-extremes ideation technique, as a first step you might push a known technique or class of techniques to an extreme. For example, you might ask yourself how you could take role playing to an extreme. The fantasy target market wishing exercise is certainly a role-play technique taken to an extreme. What else could you do? How about role-playing an animal? Or a product? Or a superhero? To make the technique even more extreme, you could combine it with another technique, let's say questioning

assumptions, to create the superhero questioning assumptions ideation technique. How different might your team's next strategic planning ideation session be if you had the Flash or Wonder Woman
questioning the assumptions behind your go-to-market strategies?

working with the 5 Ws

The five Ws is both an ideation technique and thinking approach itself,
as well as a way to prompt the invention of new techniques.

I was working with the product manager on Krazy Glue. My client,
the facilitating leader of the Krazy Glue new product development
team, saw ideation as a natural and pragmatic way to help him grow
his brand: generate some great ideas, figure out how to make and market them, and you'll grow the brand. Pretty simple.

As we talked about his wishes for the output for our new product
ideation session, we hit on a simple strategy for the session: generate
new product ideas that could achieve secondary placements in a mass-
market retailer in general and Walmart specifically. This strategy makes
a great deal of strategic sense when you have such a high share of a
particular category, as Krazy Glue did in the special-purpose glue
market. Instead of trying to steal the share from the competition, you
want to try to increase use. At the same time you're trying to increase
use, you may also want to try to increase margins by generating customized new product ideas for specific uses or niche markets.

The 5 Ws thinking strategy is about trying to use one or more of
the Ws from the reporter's formula—who, what, when, where, why,
and the outlier how—to trigger new ideation approaches and techniques. The Krazy Glue technique was about how to use a where thinking strategy to generate new product ideas. As we toured the different
Walmart departments in our imaginations, we generated dozens of
new product ideas, many of which ultimately succeeded in the marketplace. A "trip" to the jewelry department led to a high-margin jewelry
and eyeglass repair kit. In the automotive department, the group
thought of developing a new Krazy Glue that could withstand the high

temperatures associated with under-the-hood automotive repairs. In the marine department, the obvious idea was to generate a waterproof version of Krazy Glue. And in our imaginative walk through the tool section, the group was inspired to invent a new, much larger, industrial-size tube or bottle of Krazy Glue that could be used for all kinds of larger repair jobs.

So that's an example of using a where to inspire new ideas. How about a what? When we were trying to generate new positioning and new product ideas for Snuggle fabric softener, our what was the five senses. Obviously fabric softeners appeal primarily to two of the five senses: smell and feel or touch. There have been dozens of line extensions in fabric softeners offering new smells. But what about creating new products that offered different tactile, or "feel," results for different kinds of clothes or, say, bed sheets? How about leveraging the sense of hearing? Do superfresh clothes make a different sound from those that aren't? Taste is going to be tough, but how about adding an entirely new visual component to fabric softeners?

Other Ws can also provide creative inspiration. Continually asking "Why?" of a new business strategy can help identify new and important strategic intents and opportunities. Creatively asking "How?" can help you create new engineering and design ideation techniques. And "When?" could lead you to targeting particular times of the day or year (for example, different seasons) for brand-extending new products—or it could engender new ways to use or think about trends and future technologies. In new product ideation sessions for everything from locks to golf carts to cell phones, we have used not only preproduct research and technological breakthroughs as stimuli (all available through Internet searches) to trigger new ideas, but also the best new product thinking of futurists. *Futurist* magazine, for instance, not only contains stories of projected technological breakthroughs; it often polls leading technological futurists to help project when and how a new technology might affect a particular industry. For example, we have facilitated several ideation sessions on what impact telematics will have in industries as diverse as the manufacturing of heavy moving equipment and auto insurance. Telematics is a class of technologies that integrate information feedback systems with the latest technological advances (like global positioning systems) to provide performance measures. In the world of heavy moving equipment, for instance, telematics technology might help the equipment owner prevent theft (with constant tracking of the machine), continually monitor employee work performance, or provide alerts when different systems need repairs or preventive maintenance. In the world of auto insurance, telematics creates an opportunity for insurance companies to create customized auto insurance policies based on the actual driving behavior of each individual driver. Parents can monitor where their children are driving, and even how safely. Real-time, computer-analyzed, satellite-relayed feedback on speed, braking, and even if a child is doing high-speed doughnuts in the high school parking lot should revolutionize safe driving programs, not to mention auto insurance pricing models. For the facilitating leader who subscribes to the notion that the best way to know the future is to invent it, using publicly available technology triggers, it won't so much be a matter of if but when.

Inventing an ideation technique using the five Ws as creative inspiration is all about finding ways to trigger the group's creativity with more and better creative questions. And even if you don't think of it as a technique per se, one very simple way to ensure you're channeling the group's creative thinking against the appropriate strategic opportunity areas is to create a series of specific, creative questions for subteams in the ideation session to answer. How can you ensure you'll generate a broad and creative enough range of these questions to stimulate the group's creative thinking? It's simple. Make sure you have a variety of questions that begin with *who, what, when, where, why,* and *how.*

combining techniques

Probably the most obvious way to invent new ideation processes is to start by combining techniques. And the easiest technique to combine other techniques with is brainwalking. For instance, if you're not planning to do the worst idea technique by itself in the ideation session, you might include it as a rotation in the brainwalk. If you're doing a brand positioning or promotion session, consider passing out expressions from the headliner alternative technique to inspire new thinking and new ideas in one of the brainwalk rotations. Or maybe you'll want to start the brainwalk technique with a target-market wishing exercise or trigger, so you'll be sure to get new and different thinking right away. Selecting picture prompts and posting them around the brainwalking ideation stations also works. If you have the time, you could have participants do the magazine rip-and-rap exercise and post their "rips" around the brainwalk ideation stations.

One of the techniques and combination strategies I haven't yet mentioned is leveraging the work of your R&D department. They may be exploring exciting new areas of research, and it's important to take advantage of this work, even if it's in the early stages, in your ideation sessions. You could have R&D create short thought starter summary sheets on the work they are doing. These sheets could include:

- Descriptions, new forms, benefits, or mechanisms of action of unique ingredients
- Compelling product claims or product stories
- Recent technological discoveries in the industry
- Trends in their product categories
- Wishes and holy grails in their product category
- Questions or things R&D might be thinking about

To help make R&D's work be that much more effective as ideation technique triggers, we often ask a member of the R&D or product formulation team to prepare and present short thought starter presentations lasting five to ten minutes.

So the combining-techniques strategy may be less about trying to mash two techniques together to create an entirely new technique than thinking about your ultimate creative objective, and choreographing two or more techniques in a kind of one-two creative punch to achieve that objective. A good example of this was a companywide culture change initiative I worked on with Jo Tyler, now associate professor of training and organization development at Penn State, but formerly head of organization and management development at an old-line, internationally famous, but also small-town-culture American manufacturing company. In this case, we combined three creative techniques to achieve the desired result. I'll describe what we did in detail to give you a sense of why the technique-combining strategy was the right choice for ideating Jo's culture change initiative.

Jo had been recruited by the new CEO of this low-tech manufacturing firm to help transform the mind-set of the company's employees from a sleepy U.S. industry leader into a more innovative international competitor. Jo's one-on-one interviews with all levels of company employees quickly revealed what the cultural and business challenge was: the employees were killing each other with kindness. These were small-town, salt-of-the-earth, sensitive, and caring people who were reluctant at all levels of management to deliver any kind of bad or negative news about an employee's performance. Employees were not getting the kinds of constructive criticism they needed to grow as individuals or help the company challenge its own thinking and ways of doing business to become more innovative. Jo's job was to figure out a way to change this.

This is not an easy challenge. You're talking about changing company norms in a dramatic way, and changing mind-sets and behavior. These have their roots not only in an organization's long and storied history, but in the way that people were brought up in their families, communities, and even their churches.

What was Jo's way in? When Jo does culture change and organizational development work, she looks for what she calls "levers": concrete systems, processes, instruments, or procedures that can be the focal point for her programs, which are designed to help lead to "profound and healthy changes in the human condition within the organization." The lever is important because it gives the organization something concrete to focus on and change. But the lever has very little to do with Jo's real goal: creating meaningful and lasting change in employees' attitudes and behaviors.

Jo's lever for encouraging managers to give more honest feedback to their direct reports at the small-town, low-tech manufacturer was the company's performance management system. The company had an employee rating system of 1 to 10, <u>where a rating of 1 meant average</u>! That means there was no mechanism for giving an employee a below-average performance rating. If you're thinking this was not that different from the imaginary Lake Wobegon, "where all the women are strong, all the men are good looking, and all the children are above average," you would not be far off the mark. This system made it easy for managers to avoid the difficult (but nevertheless honest) conversations with their underperforming direct reports. Not only was avoiding difficult conversations bad for the company; it hurt the underperforming employees as well. Many long-time employees found themselves relegated to dead-end jobs and not having a clue as to why they weren't measuring up.

Jo immediately changed the performance management scale from the 1 to 10 rating system to a simple, three-point scale where a rating of 1 meant the employee was performing below expectations, a rating of 2 meant the employee was meeting expectations, and a rating of 3 meant the employee was exceeding expectations.

Of course, changing a process like the performance management system is only a small part of the organizational and behavioral change process. Just because there was now a new metric that encouraged more honest employee feedback and evaluations, it didn't mean that senior managers would use it honestly.

To train managers in how to give more honest feedback, Jo asked me and another organizational development friend of hers to create a two-and-a-half-day training program. So we holed up for several days, determined that we would not leave until we had designed the entire program. We called the workshop that we created—and that eleven hundred of the company's managers from around the world (including the CEO and president) wound up taking—"Dialogue: The Quest for

Candor." The workshop is a good example of the power of combining techniques in a holistic way to achieve a result that one technique could not by itself.

Three of the techniques and training exercises that we created for the workshop were the future-life collage, blind feedback, and the talking stick. We also built into the workshop the very tactical who, what, when, where, why, and how of filling out the performance management system and behavioral change tools.

From my work using collaging with consumers as an insight tool, I felt confident that a collage could be a quick way in to help elicit insights, and even profound truths, for employees as well. I knew that having senior managers create a collage is risky: it could be perceived as childish, too touchy-feely, or simply a waste of time. The fact that the CEO and president were willing to go along with this exercise said a great deal about them and their willingness to trust Jo in her effort to transform the culture of the organization. We framed the collaging exercise in the following way: "It's five years from now. You're happy with your work. What does this look like?"

The future life collage exercise achieved exactly what we hoped it would, and even more. People were able to reveal important truths about what they were wishing for and missing in their current jobs. Many also came to profound conclusions about how they would like to achieve a better work–life balance. As a way to start a dialogue with their coworkers that was indeed filled with candor, we couldn't have picked a better kickoff exercise.

We continued to leverage the richness of the collages by having the workshop participants identify the themes that they were seeing across many of the other collages. As a result, the managers began to both imagine and accept the future possibilities that both they and their coworkers were envisioning for their organization. Very powerful indeed!

Next we constructed an exercise called "blind feedback" to demonstrate how being honest can improve performance. Using children's blocks as our teaching tool, the objective of the exercise was to assemble the blocks in such a way as to create the highest tower possible. The builders were blindfolded and assigned to one of four teams. The coachers were also divided into four teams and asked to give one (and only one) form of feedback:

- No feedback at all
- Only positive feedback when the builders were doing something right
- Only negative feedback when the builders were doing something wrong or less than optimal
- Both positive and negative feedback

It probably wouldn't surprise you to learn that without exception, it was the combination of both positive and negative feedback that yielded the highest towers by far. It was a powerful metaphor, and the message was obvious to everyone in the room: if the organization were ever going to reach its true potential and achieve "the greatest possible heights," it would require its team members to give both positive and negative feedback.

Throughout the entire session, we continually made the connection back to the new performance assessment tool to be sure the participants were linking their training in candor with giving honest feedback on the tool.

The last exercise we created turned out to be a wonderful way to conclude and reinforce the theme of the workshop. Many years before, Jo had met a Lakota chief who told her about the talking stick. It is used in Native American ceremonies to give anyone in the ceremonial circle the opportunity to speak the truth from their heart. Jo had the idea to use this Native American ceremonial tool in the workshop. The talking stick exercise encouraged the session participants to share what was most important to them personally about the workshop. Interestingly, a measure of the success of the workshop was not so much what was said, as dramatic, truthful, and incredibly heartfelt as many of the comments were. Even more important was what was not said. Not one of the eleven hundred managers who took the course said what was most important was learning how to administer the performance management and behavioral change tools and interviews. The learning was far deeper than just filling out the form. It was about changing attitudes and behaviors at a very deep level.

The importance of Jo's story for facilitating leaders is that combining techniques encourages a more holistic strategy and approach for addressing the most difficult kinds of organizational challenges. You may not be able to achieve your objective, especially if you are trying to change behavior, with just one creative technique. Sometimes it takes a village of techniques.

creating a success footprint

"I realize that this isn't necessarily your area of expertise," said the marketing vice president at a major packaged goods firm, "but since you specialize in creativity and creative ideas, I thought you could help me with a meeting I'm doing with 150 of our marketing, R&D, and marketing research people. I've got a couple of hours after the day's marketing presentations and would like you to do a group activity that would be creative, fun, and energizing for the brand teams. Any ideas?"

"Let me call you back," I immediately said, which is always a good response when you have absolutely no idea what to recommend.

Two hours. One-hundred fifty people. Creative. Fun. Energizing. Not easy. Add to the creative challenge that these were not, by any stretch of the imagination, unsophisticated or inexperienced people. Somehow playing marketing story telephone, or a team competition to pass tennis balls the fastest, or even a company version of *Survivor* or *Celebrity Apprentice* was not going to cut it.

I thought about the challenge for a night and a day and wasn't getting much, but the marketing vice president needed an answer. I decided to use a creative thinking trick or strategy that I often turn to when I'm creatively stuck. Rather than trying to think of the answer, I instead think about the characteristics of the answer. The way I do it is to pretend that I've already thought of a great idea and then begin to imagine how that great idea makes me feel. With the feeling firmly in place in my mind, I start asking questions that will help me identify the characteristics of the winning idea. What makes my imagined idea so great? Why does it feel so much better than other team participation ideas? What specifically is it about the imagined idea that gives me goose bumps?

A consultant might call this approach "success factor identification." I prefer to think of it as creating a kind of success footprint. As I identify the characteristics of the as-yet-unidentified winning idea, a kind of footprint in the sand, at least in my mind's eye, begins to take shape. And while I can't yet see the actual foot (the idea) that will perfectly match that footprint, I can get a pretty good idea of what its size, shape, and weight will be from the imprint.

Identifying the idea's success footprint serves three major creative purposes:

1. It supplies the creative mind with specific triggers to creatively inspire potentially winning, focused ideas.
2. It encourages the creative mind to not give up too early or even settle for a less-than-great idea.
3. It provides a mechanism for judging which ideas are the best.

Actor and Monty Python alumnus John Cleese once said, when asked about his comedic writing success, that he tried harder than most others. He would never settle for the first idea but instead look for the second, third, or fourth idea. More ideas led to better quality. Knowing what you're looking for or, better yet, having a sense of what you're looking for, when there's no way of knowing specifically what it is, is one key to creative success.

Creative persistence is another. Creative persistence can be fueled by this feeling of knowing what you're looking for. It can also be fueled by self-confidence. Because you've solved things creatively in the past, you know you can do it again. You also know, in your heart of hearts, that there's an answer. It's already there. You've just got to keep working at it until you find it. When Thomas Edison took on the creative challenge of inventing the first practical incandescent bulb, he told the press that he'd invent it in a week—no lack of self-confidence there for the Wizard of Menlo Park. The fact that it took him and his team over a year is a testament to his creative persistence engendered in part because he intuitively knew there was an answer. Having staked his inventive reputation by bragging to the press that he'd be the one to invent the first practical electric light bulb probably didn't hurt his motivation either.

All this leads to one simple truth about creativity: it's a self-fulfilling prophecy. If you define yourself as creative, are motivated strongly enough, and persist long enough to generate a host of creative ideas, then the prophecy comes true. You are indeed creative. You've got the ideas to prove it. The problem is that a great many people simply don't define themselves as creative, and they give up too quickly. Being "uncreative" is as much a self-fulfilling prophecy as being creative. Let me repeat what Henry Ford once said: "If you think you will be a failure or success, either way you're right."

Having defined myself as creative some time ago, I set about the task of getting an idea for the group activity. One component or characteristic of my success footprint that kept coming back to me was a feeling of fun, so I did a creative thought experiment around fun. What's fun: Roller coasters? The Mardi Gras? A magic act? Luaus? Rock concerts? Stand-up comedy? Beach volleyball? Halloween? And how do we make this fun event tie into the company's brands in a creative way?

Could we have each team make a Halloween costume for their brand, or maybe even a character or personality? If one of the company's body wash brands were a famous person, living or dead, who would it be? Forget it. Stupid idea.

Could we have the teams create a stand-up comedy act around their brands? Did you hear the one about the priest, the rabbi, and the detergent? Fun, but too hard. These people weren't comedy writers.

How about if we hired magicians to come in and teach each brand team a different magic trick with its brand as the prop? Or maybe we could saw the marketing vice president in half, or better yet, have him magically disappear. Not a bad idea. Could be fun. But probably not a strong enough connection to the brands.

I decided to sleep on it.

The next morning I awoke thinking about a friend of mine, songwriter, musician, talent agent, and record producer Larry Siegel. I remembered Larry once telling me he'd sometimes teach different groups how to write a song. *Maybe*, I thought, *we have the brand teams write a song about their brand.*

I liked the idea, but a couple of things concerned me. We didn't have much time for the activity, and these people weren't songwriters. How could we rig the game to help them succeed? The answer I came up with was to provide them with the lyrics and music of songs they knew and get them to rewrite the songs with lyrics about their brand. What songs could we provide? Well-known Christmas songs (it was the holidays), rock songs, country and western, and others are all available on the Internet.

Larry liked the idea. The client liked the idea. I liked the idea. We had a gig.

The day of the event, Larry began by having the entire group write a song together about skin care. People shouted out ideas, rhymes, and refrains to Larry's prompts, and I wrote the lyrics down on an overhead projector. Pretty soon we had a fairly stupid but fun song. Guitar in hand, Larry performed the song in four different styles: rock, reggae, country western, and a kind of polka thing. The vice president of R&D came up to me after Larry's four different renditions of the skin song and said, "I'd trade everything I know to be able to do that." It was starting to feel pretty good, but the true test of the idea was still to come.

Now that we were suitably trained in some of the mechanics of writing a song, I had the group form seventeen brand teams of eight to ten people each. I gave each team lyrics from a wide variety of songs and even lists of words that rhymed with their particular brand. Each team had a little over an hour to write its song, and then just a few minutes to practice it with Larry, who was running from group to group and accompanying them on his guitar.

Over dinner, we had each team go onstage and perform their song. And of course we had all kinds of prizes in different categories, including best song, best performance, and most humorous.

I was amazed with the results. I thought that the most important learning from the exercise would be new insights on their brands. What style of music did they match with their brand's personality? What were some of the brand's equities, benefits, and features that they included in their songs? What might this mean about how they communicated their brands to consumers? And, yes indeed, this happened.

I also thought they would enjoy working and interacting with their teammates in such a fun and novel way. And this, too, happened.

But what seems so obvious now, but surprised me at the time, was the effect of the performances themselves: each team having to get up and perform their song, live, in front of an audience of 150 of their coworkers. It was their performances, not their songs, that made the event so much fun.

The performances were at once profound and silly, interesting and irrelevant, proud and embarrassing, highly competitive and entirely supportive. Everyone was smiling. Everyone was laughing. There was a childlike joy in the writing but especially in the performing. Creating and performing something with others can be a powerful bonding experience.

And it's so wonderful when people at work can see a creative side of a coworker they have never seen before. I'll never forget one manager, a staid British fellow, getting out in front of his group, strutting around like Mick Jagger singing his brand song to the music of the Rolling Stones's "Satisfaction."

I don't think it's an exaggeration to say that after that night, this company was never quite the same. Years later, people still tell me that that night was a turning point of sorts after a difficult and demotivating reorganization. It brought these wonderful people back together as a team and as a division and helped them rediscover a spirit and energy for their work that some of them had lost.

It made me feel pretty good, too. Creating an idea that can have this kind of positive, humanizing impact is pretty rewarding. And it's not a bad goal, or success footprint, for the facilitating leader in all of us.

Having a success footprint is a wonderful way of both focusing and liberating your creative mind all at the same time. Creating a success footprint also helps ensure that the ideation techniques you are creating are specifically designed to address a particular creative challenge. After all, you're not inventing new ideation techniques just for the fun of it, although it certainly is fun. Nor are you inventing new techniques just to be different, although different can be important, especially if you have a team of very experienced ideators. At the end of the day, you are inventing new ideation techniques to generate exciting new ideas for a specific business challenge.

A final word of advice if you hit a wall trying to invent a new technique, even after you've created a success footprint. Try using the semantic intuition technique (see Chapters Three and Eight) to help you. In column 1, list words that relate to your creative challenge. In column 2, list different classes of creative techniques (see Chapter Two): questioning, metaphors, visuals, brainwalking, wishing, role play, and fantasy. And in column 3, list some of the more than two dozen techniques I mention in this book. I think you'll be excited with the result!

conclusion

Some years back, my partner, Gary Fraser, and I wrote an article on what we called the total innovation enterprise, or TIE for short.[1] The basic premise of the piece is that all departments and all levels in an organization should be innovative, constantly searching, reaching, and innovating a better way. Whether you are in accounting or R&D, are the CEO or on the shop floor, everyone has a creative contribution to make. And it is my bias and my belief that the organizations that are best leveraging the innovative thinking of their employees are the ones that will thrive and win in the world's competitive marketplace. In our article, we identified ten principles that we feel embody the philosophy and essence of what it takes to be a total innovation enterprise. They also embody the underlying philosophy of this book and the spirit in which I hope it will be read and used. Here are the TIE principles.

1. *There exists an opportunity to exploit the enterprise's unrealized innovative capability.* Every enterprise has within it an extraordinary capacity to innovate. This unrealized innovative potential must be recognized and developed.
2. *Innovation opportunities are everywhere.* The whole enterprise needs to embrace innovation; it should not be the purview of just a few.

3. *Human creative potential is to be embraced.* All employees, at all levels, have the potential to make important creative contributions to the enterprise. It is wasteful to allow that potential to lie fallow.

4. *An inspired, higher-order company, department, or team vision liberates growth potential.* An inspired vision can, paradoxically, both focus and liberate the creative thinking necessary to realize the enterprise's growth opportunities.

5. *Ideas drive growth.* Ideas are the lifeblood of growth and profitability; therefore, they must be recognized, nurtured, and welcomed.

6. *Implementation is key, and it requires commitment.* Moving ideas from creation to fruition is time-consuming and difficult; the path is rife with frustration and unproductive dead-ends. The enterprise must get comfortable with the inherent difficulties and messiness of innovation.

7. *Creativity and ideation drive attitudinal and cultural change.* The act of creating and implementing ideas engenders tremendous enthusiasm, energy, and loyalty. This, not management fads and cute slogans, is what changes attitudes and culture. It is therefore essential that people be encouraged to contribute to both the ideation and innovation processes.

8. *A team's unique power to create and innovate must be understood and celebrated.* While some ideas are the eurekas of individuals working alone, cross-functional teams have their own unique abilities to create, and they are absolutely necessary to develop ideas into concrete innovations. The quality of creative energy in a group goes beyond individual capabilities—a whole greater than the sum of a team's parts.

9. *Pockets of passion are the incubators of successful innovation.* It's important to identify areas in the enterprise where true innovation is passionately demonstrated; and then develop the new, more innovative enterprise from those cores.

10. *It is essential to seek outside partners in the search for ideas.* Being too inwardly focused can be tremendously limiting. The best ideas may reside outside the enterprise, including among your network

of distributors, customers, and suppliers and in the broader market of consumers. Continually tap into those outside resources to maximize ideation and innovation potential.

The TIE is obviously an ideal: an organization that leverages creativity for growth in the most clever and important ways. At the heart of the TIE is the facilitating leader: you. I hope the techniques, tools, stories, and thinking strategies throughout this book will prove useful to you as a facilitating leader—whether for yourself, your team, or your company. This book has intentionally been written in an approachable, friendly, and creative way so that you will feel comfortable applying what you've learned. If you give these creative mind-sets, thinking strategies, ideation techniques, and innovation processes a chance, they will work. They certainly have for me, my colleagues, and our clients.

Will you actually use what's in these pages? As I ask, I'm reminded of my first trip to France when I was in college. To fulfill my language requirement at Dartmouth, I spent a term at Dartmouth's French school in Bourges, France. I was living with a French family, none of whom spoke any English whatsoever. My French "mother" picked me up at the Bourges train station (she was holding up a picture of me so we could find one another). And although I had already taken four years of French in high school, I was scared to death to speak the language with a "real French person." I'm making hand signals; she's speaking in French, slowly, with me understanding very little. I couldn't bring myself even to attempt speaking the language because I was afraid everyone would laugh at me. I'd thought I'd look and sound stupid—a very embarrassing American. It was only out of sheer desperation (I really wanted some of her delicious-looking French cooking) that I gave speaking in French a shot. And of course, after that, everything changed dramatically for the better. I had a fantastic experience—a term filled with both learning and fun. But it couldn't really begin until I was willing to push past my fear of looking (or sounding) foolish.

My experience of being afraid to speak French in France could be analogous to the predicament of an aspiring facilitating leader reluctant to experiment with the ideation techniques and innovation processes in this book. I urge you to do it in spite of your reservations. Try these techniques and processes with your team, and I bet you'll discover that the people around you will be very supportive; no matter how poorly you facilitate the techniques, they'll still work; with practice, you'll get better and more confident using the techniques; and you'll start to have fun while making significant contributions to your company. So give it a try, *mon ami!*

notes

Chapter 1

1. B. Mattimore, *99% Inspiration* (New York: AMACOM, 1994).

Chapter 2

1. J. Scully, keynote address at the Prepared Foods/Mintel New Products Conference, Sept. 2010, Palm Beach, Fla.
2. T. Kuhn, *Structure of Scientific Revolutions* (Chicago: University of Chicago Press, 1970).

Chapter 3

1. The theory and practice of the brainwalking technique is covered extensively in Chapter One. Chapter Eight also shows how brainwalking could be incorporated into a new product ideation session.

Chapter 4

1. C. Christensen, *The Innovator's Dilemma* (New York: HarperBusiness, 2011).

Chapter 5

1. A. Spelling and J. Graham, *A Prime Time Life* (New York: St. Martin's Press, 2002).

Chapter 6

1. P. Dusenberry, *Then We Set His Hair on Fire* (New York: Portfolio, 2005).

Conclusion

1. B. Mattimore and G. Fraser, "Creating a Total Innovation Enterprise," www.growth-engine.com.

acknowledgments

I have five groups of people to thank for helping me create this book: Growth Engine clients and suppliers; creativity and innovation consulting colleagues; my Growth Engine coworkers; friends; and, of course, family. Happily, these groups are not mutually exclusive.

The clients first. Pete Rollins, senior vice president from Bimbo Bakeries, deserves special mention. Pete has been supportive of Growth Engine's work for almost a decade now. In particular, when he was the general manager at Thomas' English Muffins many years ago, Pete, along with his marketing vice president, Pankaj Talwar, allowed us to pioneer the creation of Growth Engine's innovation agency concept: working very closely on an ongoing basis with him and his team to create new product successes. In the early days in particular, this was the chance my partner, Gary Fraser, and I needed to test our ideas and approaches to innovation in a real-world environment. Both Gary and I are forever in Pete's debt.

Other clients at Entenmann's, Arnold, Freihofer's, Thomas', Stroehmann, and Sara Lee—all of them now owned by Bimbo

Bakeries—have helped us develop and fine-tune our approaches and practices as well. Carl Wermers, Joe Morrissey, John Marcoux, Chris Steiner, Richard Link, Fernando Sanchez, Ted Swain, Pat Curcio, Kathleen Robbins, Lorraine Hale, Steve Zamichow, John McDonald, Weizhu Yu, Barry Frake, and Abby Prior have all been great partners in a wide variety of innovation projects.

I also thank several clients for letting me share the case studies from our work together: Tara Sexton from IBM; Dane Unger from Unger Enterprises; Joe Tyler, now a professor at Penn State; Andrea Mulhall of Danaher; Dave Moran and Patrick Meyer, formerly of Fusion 5; Allan Feldman from LMCA; Janet Lyons, founder of New Think Creative; and Hans Peter Knudsen of Rosario University in Bogotà, Colombia.

Other clients who have made Growth Engine's innovation consulting work so much fun in so many different product and service categories include Matt Smith from Bauer Hockey; Sharon DiFelice from Crayola; Jim Brown, formerly of Honeywell; Emily Liu, Katie Butler, Nola Bueno, Eric Klein, and Mikhail Chapnik from Kraft; Andy Coccari, Scott Rice, and Aaron Bethlenfalvy from Cannondale; Tim Ruth from AT&T Mobility; Eileen Corr, Tanya Laidlaw, and Nataly Avila from L'Oréal; Jim Mackey, Charlie Lundy, Harold Howlett, Chris Cortina, Jamie Burg-Travis, Nikki Arvanites, and Steve Neumann from Merck; Kristen Budney, Beth Rothman, and Lori Gertzog from Sun Products; Annamarie de la Cruz from WeightWatchers; Scot Posner, Jennifer Cole, and Doug Magnolia from BNY Mellon; Liz Kenny from Zotos; Katty Pien from Energizer; Lauren Cenzano from Esselte; Doug Curry, formerly of Schick; Beth Sweetland-Bailey from Mapfre Insurance; Adrian Bing-Zaremba from Boehringer-Ingelheim; Isser Gallogly from NYU Stern; Trish Cardin, formerly of Chicago Metallic; Jim Lawenda, now at Campbell's; Michael Simon from Panera; and Adam Rockmore from Capital Cities/ABC.

My company doesn't do much ideation and innovation training. However, there are two notable exceptions, both of which we have worked with now for over a dozen years: LVMH and the City of

New York. Thanks to Eyde Steinberg and Emma Ancelle from LVMH and Barbara Grossman and Mallory Jones from the Leadership Institute and Management Academy from the City of New York for letting us invent and field-test new approaches to ideation and innovation training.

Next, I acknowledge my Growth Engine coworkers. My partner, Gary Fraser, as you will see from several of the stories in this book, has had a key role in the creation, development, and validation of much of the intellectual property I share in this book. The fact that Gary and I are so aligned in our leadership and management philosophies, creative approaches, not to mention our business and life ethics, has made for a wonderful and frankly magical partnership that neither one of us could have imagined or realistically hoped for when we started the Growth Engine Company thirteen years ago. Having such a talented group of growth "engineers" to work with hasn't hurt either: Jane Snyder, who's been our loyal first employee for so many years now, Mary Lauren Factora, Elona Logue, Amanda Marino, and Rebecca Fretty. Also important to the ongoing success of Growth Engine have been our business development consultant, Ed Pietkiewicz, and our social media consultant, Ruth Gallogly, both of whom are tremendously skilled at what they do.

Suppliers to Growth Engine clients, as well as creativity and innovation consultants, have made important contributions to this book by referring us to new client challenges, sharing their ideas and methodologies, and being willing to experiment with our sometimes crazy ideas. Thanks to Bob Taraschi of Milestone Ideas; Julie Landy of Integer; Hugh Montgomery of HMS Design; Andy Hertz of New Directions; Elfie Campbell; Pat Schneider of Expert Access; Brian Barton of New England Marketing; Mark Polan of Polan Wasky; Liz Levy Navarro of Orrington Strategies; Kip Meyer of the IESE Business School; Leo Flanagan of Flanagan Consulting; Marty and Margie Edlesten and Brian Kurtz of Boardroom Reports; Paul Bennett of Blue Marlin; Ilene Patasnik; Mark Haffner; David Ingerman; Peter Klein; Judy Glaser of Benchmark Communications; David Snyder of Snyder Advertising; Louise

Korver; Cindi Goldberg; songwriter and musician Larry Siegel; and photographer Tim Geaney. The three creativity authors I want to thank in particular for being supportive of my work are Michael Michalko, Chic Thompsen, and Roger von Oech.

Finally, there are the friends and family who have been willing guinea pigs for sampling new products, innovative naming contributors, as well as creative sounding boards for new ideation and innovation methodologies: my wife, Hazel, who is the best new product namer I know; my sister-in-law, Trish, who has been our lead technographer (electronic meeting note taker) for over fifteen years; son James and his baseball team; daughters Caroline and Cathryn; their cousins Molly, Tommy, Meghan, Mike, and Gary; my twin sister Karen and Beijing-based brother Pat; Tracy and Jack Chester; Mary White; Sami Clyde; Bonnie and Paul Verses; Roy Rowan; Ken Schwartz; Art Shulman; Charlie Ernst; Beau, Abby, and Bob Vitanza; the Archers, the Sweeneys, and the Breunichs; Mark Richardson; Mary Carroll Moore; Sri Harold Klemp; Rhonda Stapleton; Dick Ridington; Hilary Nichols; Barbara Milnes; and Joanie Foberg.

Finally, I thank my agents, Denise Marcil and Anne Marie O'Farrell, who are talented whole-brained thinkers, handling both the creative and business side of agenting so seamlessly; and my editors at Jossey-Bass: Genoveva Llosa and Clancy Drake, who not only helped me structure this book but also pushed me to create and be explicit about teaching moments in the manuscript (which happily forced me to sharpen my own thinking) and even suggested edits that were, get this, in my own voice! Wow!

about the author

Bryan W. Mattimore is cofounder of the Growth Engine Company, a thirteen-year-old innovation agency based in Norwalk, Connecticut. Prior to cofounding Growth Engine, he was president of the Mattimore Group, a twenty-year-old ideation facilitation and creativity consulting company.

He has facilitated over a thousand brainstorming sessions, moderated over five hundred creative focus groups and consumer ethnographies, and managed over two hundred innovation projects, leading to over $3 billion in new sales for a wide variety of Fortune 500 clients, including Kraft, Unilever, Ford, AT&T, L'Oréal, Johnson and Johnson, BNY Mellon, LVMH, Merck, Pepsi, Honeywell, and Time Warner. A cum laude graduate of Dartmouth College, where he majored in psychology, he is also the inventor of the creativity training game Bright Ideas. He lives in Stamford, Connecticut, with his wife and three children and enjoys playing platform tennis in the fall and winter.

index